TEXAS
IN
REVOLT

TEXAS INDEPENDENCE FIGHTER IN 1836

TEXAS
IN
REVOLT

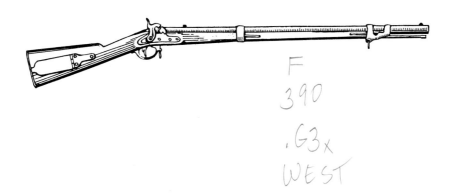

Contemporary Newspaper Account

of the

TEXAS REVOLUTION

compiled by

Jerry J. Gaddy

illustrated by

J. Hefter

THE OLD ARMY PRESS
405 LINK LANE
FT. COLLINS, COLO. 80521

*THIS BOOK IS RESPECTFULLY DEDICATED
TO THE EDITORS AND PUBLISHERS OF
ALL NEWSPAPERS*

MEXICAN SARGEANT, MATAMORAS BATTALION IN TEXAS, 1836

CONTENTS

Introduction 1

Phase No. 1 "The Country Remains Quiet". 3

Phase No. 2 "I Can Only Regard You as Rebels and Traitors". 23

Phase No. 3 "Colonel Travis has Acted Nobly and Spiritedly". 39

Phase No. 4 "The Whole Country was in Motion 73

Phase No. 5 "There is the Enemy. Do You Want to Fight?" 81

Phase No. 6 "March! To Avenge God! Your Country! And Your
            President!" 97

Phase No. 7 "....The People are Quietly Cultivating their Land." . . . 113

About the Artist 137

Acknowledgements 138

ILLUSTRATIONS

Texas Independence Fighter . . . . Frontispiece

Mexican Sargeant, Matamoras Battalion . . . . Opposite page 1

Santa Anna and His Staff on the Day Before the Assault
    and Capture of the Alamo, March 6, 1836 56

The Alamo, 5 A.M. 57

The Alamo, 8 A.M. 60

San Jacinto, 21 April 1836 61

INTRODUCTION

Anyone who has searched contemporary newspapers instantly recognizes the immense value of this book. Contemporary newspapers give an on-the-spot type of history, printed while the events were happening. They reflect the feeling of the moment, as opposed to considered judgement after all the facts are in. Very often it is this "feeling of the moment" that the reader or researcher is trying to capture. *Texas in Revolt* lets you see the Texas Revolution as contemporary Americans saw it; as it happened.

The Troy Daily Whig reported the news of the fall of the Alamo to its readers two months after the event. It was news in New York. A look at these invaluable news accounts explains why Texas received help from the United States, and often explains attitudes of the various sections of the country. The Texas Revolution was real to Americans throughout the country, as real as Vietnam is to you today. They had but one media to obtain news - the printed page. Newspapers meant much more in the daily life of the 1830's than they do today.

Through the tireless efforts of Jerry Gaddy, you can, in this single volume read accounts from around the nation. Those of you who have spent the countless hours tracking down the location of a certain newspaper, then waited more countless weeks for a reproduction, can appreciate Jerry's labors. Everyone can enjoy *Texas in Revolt*. Thanks to Jerry Gaddy, accounts from every section of the United States have been gathered together in this single volume. The

1

accounts have not been edited, nor corrected, for to do so would destroy not only their charm, but impair their value. There are numerous good books on the Texas Revolution. Only one was written by so many people, giving so many viewpoints, as it happened - *Texas in Revolt.*

MICHAEL J. KOURY
Editor, The Old Army Press

"The Country Remains Quiet"

SANTA ANNA TAKES OVER THE MEXICAN GOVERNMENT . . . AUSTIN IS RELEASED FROM PRISON . . . TROUBLE AT ANAHUAC . . . THE CUSTOM HOUSE FIGHT . . . GENERAL COS PREPARES TO COME TO TEXAS . . . THE TEXANS PREPARE FOR TROUBLE . . . AUSTIN RETURNS FROM MEXICO . . . COS ARRIVES IN TEXAS . . . SAM HOUSTON — "WAR IN TEXAS IS INEVITABLE" . . . COS STATES THAT TEXAS IS PEACEFUL . . . VOLUNTEERS LEAVE U. S. FOR TEXAS . . . EDITORIAL SPEAKING OUT AGAINST TEXAS CAUSE . . . A PLEA FOR AID FROM TEXAS.

NEW YORK COURIER AND INQUIRER

LATEST NEWS OF THE REVOLUTION IN MEXICO
TO THE EDITOR OF THE COURIER & Inquirer:

From the enclosed newspapers you will perceive that Gen. Santa Anna and his adherents have resolved upon the destruction of the present constitution of the Republic, and the establishment in its place a consolidated military government. According to the invariable practice in such cases, measures to bring about this resolution were concerted in the city of Mexico, and the first attempts to carry them into execution made at Zacatecas and other towns when the military and a deluded populace led on by the priests have declared in favor of a despotic form of government, for such it is in reality to disguise it as they may under the name of representative government. Strong symptoms of a similar declaration have shown themselves among the garrisons of this place, Tampico and San Luis, it is well to add, however, that public opinion in this section of Mexico is decidedly opposed to the change. What effect this extraordinary resolution will have on the personal security and property of foreign residents, is impossible to foresee, especially if evident hostility of the ruling faction to foreigners in general, be borned in mind. Many of them have already experienced the grossest insults here, and according to the last accounts from Monclova, the seat of government of the State of Cohuhuila and Texas, several Americans have been very ill treated by the troops of Gen. Cos, sent thither with orders to dissolve the present Legislature. It is such to be regretted that under existing circumstances we are left without a representative at the city of Mexico. At no period was a Minister here more necessary than at the present, when so many causes combine to create an ill feeling towards American citizens residing in or visiting this country.

THE TROY DAILY WHIG

LATER FROM MEXICO

Gen. Santa Anna was expected to arrive in the city of Mexico towards the 12th of June, 1835. An attempt is positively to be made to introduce a regular government in Texas, and preparatory measures were taken at Matamoras, Monclova and Matagorda. By the Mexican papers and private advices it would appear that the principal object of the government is to suppress the contraband trade carried on through the ports of the colony; to prevent the legislature of Cohuhuila and Texas from making large grants of land and to check the operations of the American land holders or companies. It is generally supposed however, that if this attempt should be successful, which we much doubt, it will not affect, bona fide settlers.

EXTRACT OF A LETTER FROM COL. STEPHEN F. AUSTIN, TO HIS FRIEND IN TEXAS.

Mexico, 13th May, 1835

The amnesty law was published on the 3rd inst., and as it embraces my case fully, I have been trying ever since to get my bail bonds cancelled, which I am told will be done in a few days, so that I have fixed the 25th of this month to start home, in company with D. Victor Blanco, who goes as far as Monclova.

Every thing is tranquil in this part of the country, and likely so to remain; it is said today that General Santa Anna has concluded the difficulty at Zacatecas; he informed me just before his departure on that expedition that he intended to visit Texas this summer, and remedy all your wants so far as he could do; he expressed himself friendly towards Texas. It is the opinion of intelligent men here, that the federal system will not be changed, but that some reforms will be made, and that one of them perhaps will be to make a state of Texas.

I hear with great pleasure that you are all getting on in peace, and have money in Texas. Any disturbance there will be VERY unfortunate at this time. A dead calm is the best, and only proper course for Texas.

THE TROY DAILY WHIG

LATE FROM MEXICO

Extract from a letter dated city of Mexico Aug. 1st, 1835.

"The country at present is tranquil, but to advance an opinion as to how long this tranquility will continue, would be mere speculation. The present subject of discussion is whether the executive power shall revolve on Santa Anna alone, or upon a union of two others with him. Upon the settlement of this question, will depend the future tranquility of things. Santa Anna is radically opposed to any division of this power."

A letter from Vera Cruz says —

' In politics some trifling difficulties having arisen between the congress and the President, have retarded the establishment of our new system of government — in consequence of which, although we have no new troubles to fear, we still remain in a state of uncertainty, which is a great dettiment to our commercial affairs.

LATE FROM MEXICO

The Sol, a semi-official paper in the city of Mexico, gives an account of Capt. Tenorio of the Mexican army and the settlers in Texas. From this account it appears that the Mexican officer who landed at Galveston with 34 soldiers, for the purpose of protecting the Custom House officers stationed at Anahuac was taken by surprise, the account says, by the North Americans. The Custom House officers, and soldiers unable to resist their assailants, abandoned the establishment and fled in all directions. This occurance has raised the indignation of the Mexicans to such a pitch that it was rumored that in the city of Mexico, Santa Anna, himself, would go to Texas at the head of an army to put a stop to what they call, "the intrusions of the North Americans in Texas."

Capt. Fentress, of the schr. Mariner, from Matamoras, reports that during his stay there, the Mexican authorities had acted with great severity towards American citizens. They had even refused for some days to let any of our vessels leave the port, and had endeavored to persuade the seamen to join them in their projected invasion of Texas, but without success.

NEW YORK COURIER
LATEST FROM MEXICO

Latest accounts from Mexico have been received, from which it appears that Santa Anna issued his proclamation, calling for an extraordinary session of the representatives of the nation, to assemble at the City of Mexico in order to decide on the future form of the government of the republic.

Santa Anna had left the capital for his farm at Manga de Clavo, and rumor was afloat that after taking a few days rest, he would embark for Texas; but this is not probable. The forces placed at the disposal of Cos, who commands the expedition against Texas, is to be composed of three battalions of infantry, and 300 cavalry, in all 1500 men. Texas being the only state of the Republic, which far from protesting — as most of the states have done — against the present form of federal system, appears determined to preserve it; it's military occupation has been decided upon by the supreme government, thus giving some occupation to the troops and calling the attention of the Mexicans — so much excited at present by the contemplated changes in the free institutions of the country — to another quarter. The success of this enterprise appears very doubtful, especially if the Texanos are united. The Mexican government has received the alarming intelligence that Mr. Zavala — who, last year, resigned his situation of Mexican Ambassador, near the court of France, on account of his opposition to the principals of the present administration — was expected to arrive in Texas. Hence it was inferred that Mr. Zavala had in view the separation of Texas from the Mexican confederation. Mr. Zavala had no such intentions when he arrived at New Orleans from New York. All his preparations here, previously to his departure for that colony, seemed to indicate his determination to form there a settlement, and to retire to private life with his numerous family. Subsequently the conduct of the Mexican government in forbidding Mr. Zavala to go to Texas, so much exasperated this gentleman, that, far from complying with the order of the President to repair to Mexico, he openly declared his determination to oppose the despotic government of Santa Anna, and to join the people of Texas in their exerations to preserve their constitutional rights, making, at the same time, an appeal to every Mexican patriot, in order to induce them to imitate the example of a handful of North American settlers.

If I remind you of the popularity of Mr. de Zavala among his countrymen, his constant devotion to the federal system, and above all, his enterprising spirit, you will not be surprised to hear, by the first dispatch, that he has placed himself at the head of the provisional government of Texas. If, as I confidently hope, such be the case, no apprehensions ought to be entertained on the ultimate result of the struggle which is preparing in that colony!

8

NEW YORK
COURIER AND INQUIRER

PREPARATION FOR A MILITARY EXPEDITION
AGAINST TEXAS CONTINUES.

The preparation for a military expedition against Texas continues. The command was entrusted to Brigadier General Cos. We have already stated in this paper that the military occupation of this colony will meet with strong difficulties!

The disaffected in the province of Chipas has not been entirely subdued, but Col. Gil Perez, commander of the troops of Santa Ann, was not killed, as the papers from Vera Cruz had reported. He has lately obtained some advantages, but in his last report to the Minister of War, he states that he has not succeeded in destroying entirely two or three bands that disturb the tranquility of that province.

The country remains quiet.

THE NEW ORLEANS
TRUE AMERICAN
IMPORTANT FROM TEXAS!!

By the arrival of the schooner Lady Madison, Capt. Dunford from Velasco, whence she started, we are put in possession of late information from Texas. It appears that the country is in a state of extraordinary excitement and on the eve of a revolution. The alarming progress of centralism through the rest of the Mexican republic, — a threatened invasion by Santa Anna, — a meditated sale of a large quantity of land, — the imposition of burthensome taxes on the commerce of the country, and the arrest of the governor, are circumstances which have aroused the people of Texas to the defense of their rights and to resist oppression. Meetings have been held in all the towns and villages. Among the rest, Columbia, Harrisburg, Velasco, Brazoria, and San Felipe have adopted resolutions expressive of indignation at the proceedings of the General Government, and of a determination to resist them. A convention has also been called by those meetings, and a determination expressed to abide by it's decision. The Convention was to have met on the 14th Sept., 1835, and it was expected that it would take such measures as well as excite Santa Anna to prosecute his threatened invasion. It will doubtless call upon every Texonian to resist by every honorable means — remonstrances first and arms afterwards — the usurpations of Centralism.

It is stated, that all the states of Mexico, except Texas, have given their consent to Centralism to the dominion of Santa Anna. This system will doubtless be the proper one for the Mexican people, but it will not do for the Americans. Texas cannot submit to it; her only resource is in arms!! A declaration of independence is the next thing we will doubtless hear of.

Santa Anna is concentrating a large force at Saltillo. If he moves one step towards Texas, it will amount to a declaration of war!!

The political chiefs have issued proclamations for the purpose of allaying the excitement, but they are little regarded.

The Texonians look with confidence towards their fellow citizens of the United States, particulary to those of the western states. for assistance in case of war with Santa Anna. It is hoped that they will not be disappointed in this expectation. In fact we believe that at the first signal, thousands of the hardy sons of the west will cross the boundary to join their former fellow citizens in maintaining the principals of '76.

THE NEW ORLEANS TRUE AMERICAN

TEXAS

We are in possession of the proceedings of a meeting which took place in two small Districts of Texas, from which it would seem that the settlers are unwilling to submit to the political changes attempted in the system of government of the Mexican Republic, and still contemplated by the present administration. They declare their determination to resist by arms the occupations of their territory by Mexican troops, and besides threaten the Mexican government with a separation. If these proceedings are approved and acted upon by the people of Texas generally, which is very doubtful, they may together with the Captain of the Schooner Corres, induce the Mexican government to march into the province the military force which has been collecting for some time past on the frontier. It is impossible to say what effect a war between the Mexican and American settlers in Texas may have on our commercial relations with that Republic.

NEW YORK AMERICAN

IMPORTANT FROM TEXAS

We have received today from a gentleman in Texas, a letter dated the 6th of September, 1835 giving the important intelligence that a Convention was to be held on the 15th of October, composed of five members elected from each jurisdiction of the Province, to consult on the public safety, and intimating that one of its acts would be "a Declaration of Independence." The following extracts:

"The state of our affairs which have been for some time extremely threatening to our new settlement, has at last come to such a pass that leaves us no alternative but to yield our brilliant prospects with our brilliant prospects with our hard hard earnings, (obtained at a sacrifice of exile from our beloved country the United States,) to the Mexicans, or to expel them by force of arms from Texas, our adopted country. This we will do or die in the attempt. We occupy a country which but for our presence would ever have remained a wilderness, because the Mexicans were afraid to occupy a country inhabited by so many Indians; and these numerous tribes, which are settled about us in every direction, they are by spies and emissaries trying to raise to strike the first blow on the American settlers of Texas, and imbrue their murderous tomahawks in the blood of our defenceless women and children. Our particular location is more exposed than any

other, the neighborhood having settlements of North American Indians who having become dissatisfied in the United States came here several years ago. They consist principally of Cherokees, Shawnees, Kickapoos, Delawares, Coshatoes and Alabamas: and there are besides numerous small Spanish tribes, all of whom reside within 25 to 60 miles of Nacogdoches, and the two first mentioned, who are the most numerous, within twenty-five or thirty-five miles. Some of these Indians are visiting us daily to trade. Sixty horses were counted the other day in the town. These Indians always have been friendly with us, and would remain so, were it not for the infamous overtures made to them by the Commandant of the Mexican army, who has taken possession of Bejar, distant direction in which our neighboring from us 340 miles, situated in the Indians go to hunt.

"This desperate state of affairs will oblige me to change my plans. I have it in contemplation to take my family for immediate safety, to Fort Jessup, Louisiana, and leaving them there for a short time, as we have several friends in the garrison, till a more healthy season to descend Red River, and ascend the Mississippi, where in case our troubles continue, they can remain. I shall not be able to accompany them as all my future prospects are in Texas, and they

IMPORTANT FROM TEXAS
(CONTINUED)

are now most probably to be left to a state of war. The confidence which the Americans in Texas feel in their power over the Mexican troops gives them much less uneasiness than they have from their more powerful neighbors the Indians, most of whom we consider equal warriors to ourselves, while we calculate to whip the Mexican troops with great facility.

"Enclosed I send you the proceedings of a meeting at Columbia. On the 15th of October, 1835 a general Convention of Delegates from all Texas will meet, when they will declare us "Independent of Mexico." Red River is all alive to our interest, and offering us their assistance as individuals, as well as Mississippi and New Orleans, whence we look for considerable aid."

THE PENSACOLA GAZETTE

LATE AND IMPORTANT FROM TEXAS!

The most intelligent account we have yet seen of the actual position of affairs in Texas, is contained in the following recent letter from there in the Tallahassee Floridian of Oct. 10th.

The following extract of a letter, (says the Floridian) dated the 8th of Sept. 1835, on the San Jacinto River, in Texas, for which we are indebted to the politeness of a lady, will be read with deep interest. The author is a respectable gentleman personally known to most of the readers of the Floridian, in middle Florida; a witness to the scenes, and a participator of the events he describes; his narrative is entitled to the fullest credit.

LYNCHBURG, ON SAN JACINTO RIVER, TEXAS SEPTEMBER 8, 1835

"I do not think it would be prudent for you and our family to come to Texas, until the affairs of the country assume a more peaceful aspect.

St. Anna has applied to the Priests for two millions of dollars and six thousand men, to put down the Rebels of Texas, (as he styles us,) but it is in the reality to turn out the Protestants and establish the Roman Catholic Religion. We are preparing for war in every part of Texas — not partisan war but constitutional war, as did our forefathers in the Revolution.

A grand Convention is to assemble at San Felipe on the 10th of October next. The members will be something like fifty in number, from all the districts.

I have been returned a member by a large majority, in favor of entire secession and absolute independence of the Mexican Government, be it what it may — Republican Centralism, or Imperialism.

Our position is at this time extremely interesting to the United States, and in fact to all the powers of Europe, who have relations with the Mexican Government. A Provincial Government will be immed-ately formed, and a regular army of 5000 men raised and equipped to take the field.

We look upon our independence as absolutely certain. We have now the command of all the harbors in Texas, and have driven out every garrison from the interior of our fine country. Some fifteen hundred troops have been sent against us, but they have (unexpectedly) returned; being afraid to move against our riflemen, to the amount of 300 or more. They have sent to Mexico for a reinforcement, and St. Anna has pledged himself to the priests, to head the army in person. Col. Austin has just returned from Mexico, where he has been in prison for the last two years; he has united all parties. We have just received news of a victory obtained by one of our small vessels (the San Felipe) in the successful repulse and subsequent capture of the Coreco, Captain Thompson. The engagement lasted about an hour, when the naval representative of Santa Anna lowered his flag; then all the brave Mexicans having previously deserted their posts and gone down into the hole. This Thompson has been the

14

(CONTINUED)

scourge of our coast and bays. — We are now fitting up two other vessels to guard our own coast. In fact, although no war has been declared, we are in a complete state of warfare, and in six weeks expect to give the world a declaration of independence. So soon as this glorious event takes place, we shall send an agent to Washington to solicit an acknowledgement of our independence; but in the meantime, we know of at least 5000 soldiers, principally riflemen from Kentucky, Tennessee, etc. who are only waiting for the event.

Everyone who assists, whether on land or at sea, will be munificently rewarded by the Texas Republic, in the fairest land under the finest climate in the known world. I have been so much engaged lately in political meetings, committees of safety and correspondence, etc. that I have time for little else; in time the whole country is only alive to one single subject: liberty or death; for such we will get if we do not turn the tables on Santa Anna. I think the Kentucky boys will play the shaven crowns a sharp game if they take any of them: GOD SAVE THE MARK! My own affairs are going on as well as I can expect: The mill stops, of course, muster days, drill days, rejoicing days for victory, etc., but all will soon be quiet, and then we shall reap a fine harvest."

LATER STILL

By a letter received by the Philadelphia Gazette, dated Nocogdoches, Sept. 14, 1835, we are concerned to add that the people of Texas are in a great state of anxiety, in consequence of the despot — Santa Anna having excited the Indian tribes to war against the settlers. A council has been held by the tribes of the Cherokee settlement — thirty miles north of Nacogdoches, at which were some of the distant tribes of Comanches. The people of Texas have written to President Jackson to arrest the emigration of the Creeks; 5000 of whom were soon expected, and who, it was feared might be induced to join the other Indians. They also call upon their brother Americans in the north to send on munitions of war and reinforcements.

RED RIVER HERALD

HIGHLY IMPORTANT FROM TEXAS! WAR IN TEXAS! GENERAL COS LANDED NEAR THE MOUTH OF THE BRAZOS WITH 400 MEN!!

Isaac Parker has just arrived from Texas, bringing the intelligence that Gen. Cos has landed near the mouth of the Brazos River with 400 men, with the intention of joining the 700 federal troops stationed at San Antonio de Bexar, and marching upon the people of Texas. He has issued his proclamation, "declaring that he will collect the revenue, disarm the citizens, establish a military government, and confiscate the property of the rebellious." Messrs. Johnson and Baker bore the express from San Felipe to Nacogdoches. S. F. Austin has written to several citizens of Nacogdoches, that a resort to arms is inevitable.

They have hoisted a flag with "THE CONSTITUTION OF 1824" inscribed on it, and 200 freeman gathered 'round it, determined to stand or fall with it. We subjoin the following letter from General Houston to the gentleman who brought the intellignce:

San Augustine, Texas
October 5, 1835

Dear Sir — At your request I hand you a memorandum that you may be informed of our situation. War in defence of our rights, our oaths, and our constitutions is inevitable in Texas!

If volunteers from the United States will join their brethren in this section, they will receive liberal bounties of land. We have millions of acres of our best lands unchosen, and unappropriated.

Let each man come with a good rifle and one hundred rounds of ammunition, — and to come soon.

Our war cry is "LIBERTY OR DEATH!!" Our principals are to support the constitution, and down with the usurper!!

Your Friend,
Samuel Houston

TROY DAILY WHIG

MEXICO - TEXAS

Intelligence has been received at N. Y. from Mexico up to the 5th Sept., 1835. It appears that in a session of the Mexican Congress, explanations were demanded of Ministers in regard to the state of affairs in Texas. The Minister of War stated the Government had received despatches from Gen. Cos, Commander of that Dept., and that they were of a most satisfactory character. The settlers, he said, had given evidence of their firm de termination to keep the peace, and to submit to the government of the confederation. There is therefore at present no reason to suppose that there will be any further disturbance in that colony.

JOURNAL OF COMMERCE

TEXAS

Very considerable numbers of men are leaving various parts of our country for Texas, taking with them the arms and munitions nevessary for war. Some hundreds will leave the Atlantic coast within ten days, and still a larger number probably will go from the west. Santa Anna will find the Kentucky riflemen bad troops to contend with, in such a war as will be waged in Texas, and it would not be strange if take it all in all, he should find this to be the hardest job he ever undertook. If the tide of offensive operations should be turned the other way, and with such power, as to shake his arbitary authority beyond the limits of Texas, it would not be the strangest thing that ever happened.

BALTIMORE GAZETTE

TEXAS

Those who have volunteered to join the Texians, and those who may wish to do so, are requested to meet the committee at the Arcade this evening at six o'clock, for the purpose of taking measures for organizing themselves, prepatory to an immediate departure; arms and ammunition will be furnished them, and their passage paid so far as Natchitoches.

NOTE

The committee composed of Messrs. James H. Caldwell, W. Bogart, Wm. Bryan, Jas. N. Niven, Wm. S. Hodger, Thomas Banks, James Ramage, and Wm. Christy, will receive donations of muskets, rifles and ammunition. Those wishing to aid the cause by subscription can do so by application to any member of the committee.

Accustomed as we are gradually becoming to the law of the stronger, and habituated as the general government seems to be to the assumption of the highest powers by individuals, we should suppose that this outrageous manifesto, this flagrant usurpation of the right vested in the legislature of the United States to declare peace or war, would arouse them from their supineness. Here we have a knot of citizens of the United States deliberately taking measures for organizing, arming, and maintaining a force for the purpose of entering into an alliance offensive and defensive with a set of frontiersmen styling themselves Texians or Texonians, against Mexico, a peaceable government under relations of friendship with that under which we pretend to live. There has never perhaps been a sounder article of international law, nor one the moral justice of which is less questionable than that which constitutes a high and capital crime for an individual to levy war upon a government — this is the article on which Joachin Murat was condemned and shot at Naples; this is the article on which General Jackson relied, when he hung Ambrister and Arbuthnot, when we were at peace with Great Britain— both of which executions were not only just and legal, but have received the sanction of the world as such.

Now to look briefly and impartially into this matter, we shall find that there is not the slightest shadow of right on the side of the Texonians, nor on circumstance to call forth sympathy or commiseration. A party of land speculators of our large cities have cast a longing eye on the rich and fertile province of Texas, as they might have done on Andalusia, or the county of Kent, or the plains of Austrian Italy, or any other portion of the globe whatsoever which is evidently and unquestionably the property of some foreign power. These land speculators obtain tracts of land under the then constitution of this foreign country, and proceed with all the tricks and stratagems usually resorted to in such cases to induce American citizens to emigrate to their newly acquired territories. This done, and a large population of Yankees from the Eastern States, and backwoodsmen from Kentucky, Tennessee and Mississippi being established in Mexico, these aforesaid land speculators endeavor by all means to induce the general government to purchase Texas of the Mexican government.

This notable scheme fails — and the speculators then determine as a last resource to conquer the country on their own hook, calculating that when they have done so they shall be enabled to prevail on the United States to admit them to the confederation. This then is the clue to the whole matter — circumstances have caused the plot to explode a little too soon, and the engineers seem to run some risk of being "hurt by their own petards." They cannot as yet count enough American riflemen to drive the rightful lords of the soil out of their own country; and therefore they make up a pitiful face and cry oppression, and call upon individuals to shoulder their rifles and come to their aid, and inform them as an inducement to do so that they have millions of acres — of Mexican lands be it observed — which they with unequaled liberality will bestow on those who aid them to conquer them. So long as this matter rested solely with individuals we took no part in the controversy. If American citizens thought fit as individuals to go forth on this crusade, running the risk of being hanged, and acting on their own responsibility, the government could not well interfere. If these chivalrous individuals had been caught warring against the Mexican authorities, proceeded against as robbers, murderers and land pirates, and such had been ordered for execution, our government would of course have left them to their fate. Prevent them from going about their own business it could not!

This affair is now however changed in toto; Mr. Caldwell, Bogart & Co., whose principals we doubt not may be found in Wallstreet, propose organizing, arming and importing at their own or their employers expense an American force into the territories if Mexico for the avowed purpose of supporting armed rebels against a friendly power. Nay, this is not all — the San Felipe, a vessel owned, armed, freighted and navigated from the United States of America, goes out on a smuggling expedition to Texas, a province of Mexico, is very naturally and properly stopped by the Correo, a Mexican vessel of war of the revenue department, and immediately proceeds with the utmost sangfroid to capture and bring into New Orleans the Mexican revenue cutter.

With exactly the same propriety might a Baltimore clipper sail with a freight of contraband tobacco, and a heavy armament for Deal, or Dover, or any other English port, and on being stopped by the British cutter, capture her and bring her into New York or a British smuggling trader with a cargo and broadcloth, take our revenue schooners and carry them as prizes to Liverpool. It is a hard rule that will not work both ways, and if this rule were to work thus, we should be a little surprised if the affair were to end in smoke between Andrew Jackson and Great Britain.

The moment, therefore, has arrived, when the government of the United States must interfere or violate the first principles of international law. Every principle of equity, justice and morality call upon to interfere for the prevention

19

of this outrage on society — nor is this all, every principal of policy, of expediency, and self-interest.

Shall it be said of us that we exclaim and complain loudly and utter cries of indignation of a foreign nation sends her emissaries to argue with us merely and peaceably to convince us of the evils of our domestic government, and that we at the same time allow our own citizens to levy armies for the subversion of foreign powers connected with ourselves in bonds of amity? Shall it be said hereafter, when by the secret and underhand aid of American citizens, in violation of international law, acting in defence of rebels, Texas shall be disunited from its parent state and shall have been received, on the application of its conquerors into the Union, shall it be said then, that we have indeed exhibited the grasping and ambitious policy, which the enemies of popular governments attribute to the genius of republicanism, in its highest and most flagitious point of view! That we have employed secret agents to conquer for us, what for very shame, we dare not conquer openly and for ourselves?

Such must be the accusations to which we shall render ourselves liable if we do not at once openly and decidedly check this insubordinate and daring spirit. Nor are such accusations all the evil. Mexico, is, it is true, a weak state, and one whose hostility may at first sight seem little formidable to such a power as ours; yet let us remember that the sea swarms with our traders, that our commerce is far and wide, and that on our commerce depends in a great measure our public and private welfare — let us remember that even an ant may be trampled on; till it shall rise and sting the foot of the intruder — and so Mexico may sting us, and her sting may be fatally venomous. Let her issue letters of marque and interest will arm a thousand foes against our commerce; let her issue letters of marque and we must either submit to see our merchant ships swept from the ocean, or we must quadruple our naval force; and must send out cruiser after cruiser, we must fight for every cargo and we must be taxed for every battle. And for what we submit to all this evil — that we may at the present moment enrich a few land speculators, jobbers and brokers, "et hoc gemus onne" and finally endanger our own national existence. Aye, our national existence! — By every foot of land we add to the Union we weaken, we disunite, and we dissolve! Let Texas be conquered from Mexico — what then? There will be still a frontier — still a boundary line betwixt our lands and those of Mexico, and there will still be Yankee Jobbers and western Woodsmen to enroach beyond those limits — the history of Texas will be that of Mexico; the history of Mexico will be that of Gautamala; and so on till Panama and the Pacific shall be the boundaries of our restless craving, and the insatiable avarice! — "Satis superque"! Should be even now our motto — we are already well nigh too large for self-government, we already comprehend too many jarring interests! Increase to us is ruin! Like

20

the Roman Empire we shall fall to pieces imperceptibly from a mere want of moral cement to keep together our component atoms.

This is the fate which our wise men already fear; and shall we, to satisfy the madness of a miserable and interested minority, increase the cause of their apprehensions? Shall we break every international law, every moral principal, every maxim of justice, or shall we set our foot down and resolutely say to our over-bold, rebellious citizens — "We suffer no foreigner to interfere with you, nor will we suffer you to interfere with any foreigner. Your rights are guaranteed to you, and therefore you must abstain from enroaching on the rights of others?"

If any person can be found to deny the justness of this position, or the inequity of our suffering of our citizens to act as they now propose to do, we shall never in the future believe that right or reason means anything but party spirit and interested motives; but we do not believe it possible that any can be found to uphold a cause which is evidently a variance with equity and law, and more that all with the very spirit of Christianity which perscribes to us the leading maxim — "Do unto others as you would they should unto you!"

TROY DAILY WHIG

FROM TEXAS

The General Council of Texas has issued a proclamation, addressed to the citizens of the United States, setting forth the grievances of the Texans and evoking assistance. The following passages are copied from the document, as containing the substance as a whole. "Editors friendly to the cause of Texas" are requested by the General Council to copy them, and we comply with that request as holding ourselves within the terms of the invitation; we are friendly to the cause of the Texans so far as that cause is just, although we still maintain that some of the measures heretofore taken in aid of the Texans are manifestly not legal.

"What number of mercenary soldiers will invade our country we know not, but this much we do know, that the whole force of the nation that can possibly be spared will be sent to Texas, and we believe victory in the end will be ours But one sentiment animates every bosom, and all, everyone, is determined on "VICTORY OR DEATH!"

Citizens of the United States of the north, we are but one people! Our fathers, side by side, fought the revolution. We side by side, fought the battles of the war of 1812 and 1815. We were born under the same government and taught the same political creed, and we have wandered where danger and tyranny threaten us. You are united to us by all the sacred ties that can bind one people to another. You are, many of you, our fathers and our brothers — among you dwell our sisters and mothers — we are aliens to you only in country, — but principles, both moral and political are the same — our interest is one, and we require and ask your aid. and we earnestly appeal to your patriotism and generosity. WE INVITE YOU TO OUR COUNTRY — WE HAVE LAND IN ABUNDANCE, AND IT SHALL LIBERALLY BE YOURS. WE HAVE THE FINEST COUNTRY ON THE FACE OF THE GLOBE. WE INVITE YOU TO ENJOY IT WITH US, AND WE PLEDGE TO YOU, AS WE ARE AUTHORIZED TO DO, THE LANDS OF TEXAS AND THE HONOR AND FAITH OF THE PEOPLE, THAT EVERY VOLUNTEER IN OUR CAUSE SHALL NOT ONLY JUSTLY BUT GENEROUSLY BE REWARDED!

The course of Texas is plainly marked out. She shall drive every Mexican soldier beyond her limits, or the people of Texas will leave San Antonio the bones of their bodies. We will secure on a firm basis our constitutional rights and privileges, or we shall leave Texas a howling wilderness!"

"... I Can Only Regard You As Rebels And Traitors."

PHASE #2

THE BATTLE OF GONZALES . . . VOLUNTEERS LEAVE FOR TEXAS . . . MEXICAN TROOPS ORDERED TO MATAMORAS . . . THE BATTLE OF CONCEPTION . . . THE SIEGE OF BEXAR . . . TROOPS ON THE MARCH TO ASSIST THE TEXIANS . . . COS SURROUNDED AT THE ALAMO . . . TEXAS ADOPTS BILL OF RIGHTS . . . THE CAPTURE OF GOLIAD BY THE TEXIANS . . . MORE VOLUNTEERS FOR TEXAS . . . COS SURRENDERS THE ALAMO.

RED RIVER HERALD

NEWS FROM TEXAS
DEFEAT OF THE MEXICANS AT GONZALES -
THE COMMANDER SLAIN!

A dispatch from "The Camp Of The Volunteers" dated Oct. 2nd, 1835, and signed by ten of the party, calls on their American brethren for immediate aid; and that an action had taken place the day before at Gonzales, in which the Mexican commander was slain, along with several of his soldiers. No loss on the American side. A letter from Capt. John H. Moore, from Gonzales, says they have a 150 men at that more are hourly expected. He calls for more aid. The enemy were on the opposite side of the river, 200 in number and rapidly reinforcing. — Mr. W. H. Wharton, who was sent on to Brazoria to communicate more particular details, states that, the volunteers were in the highest state of spirits and health. Gen. Cos, it is said, has with him 800 pair of IRON HOBBLES for the benefit of the Americans. Mr. Wharton says, truly, "Now's the day and now's the hour," and that 500 can do more at this moment than 5000 six months from now. San Antonio can be starved into a surrender in ten days. — There are 800 Mexican troops there, and they have already created a famine among the inhabitants, who can scarcely raise enough for their own consumption. They have no bread or meat, and must soon eat their own horses, or pillage the colonists.

The object of the volunteers is to intercept Cos between Bahia and San Antonio After this our countrymen propose to take San Antonio by storm. If not taken, it will be a rallying point where thousands of the enemy's troops will concentrate. Arrangements are making in Brazoria and Matagorda, to send on provisions and ammunition, etc. Columbia and San Felipe will do the same. Mr. Wharton says he was to leave Brazoria, for the camp at Gonzales, the next day, (Oct. 4th) and urges those who are disposed to accompany him to equip themselves forthwith. Those who can follow on within 10 or 15 days, may still, he says, be of eminent service. He has no doubt there will be, in a few days, 600 American volunteers in Gonzales.

A letter of a later date from Brazoria to the Editor of the New Orleans Bulletin, says that Col. Austin's return has united all parties. Santa Anna's forces have been concentrating at Bexar, on the San Antonio river, for the past three months. Bexar is 175 miles nearly west of San Felipe. The letter goes on to say:

But the war is now begun, and ye shall know how it was commenced.

Some years since, when Gonzales, the capital of De Witt's Colony, was exposed to the depredations of the Indians, the people there applied to the authorities of Bexar for a piece of artillery to protect that frontier. The application was granted; and they obtained a brass six pounder. This was kept for defence until the settlement became strong — and afterwards it lay about the streets upon the ground, unmounted, and served to make a noise whenever

NEWS FROM TEXAS
DEFEAT OF THE MEXICANS AT GONZALES —
THE COMMANDER SLAIN!

(CONTINUED)

the people got into a merry frolic. The military commandant of Bexar, (Col. Ugartechea), feeling sufficiently strong to make an attack upon the colonies, demanded the gun. The people took the matter into consideration. The gun was once the property of the King of Spain; and he lost it with the sovereignty of the country. The Federal Republic of Mexico became the owner. The people of Gonzales returned the answer, in substance, that the gun was the property of the confederation which they acknowledged, and not the Central Government, which they did not acknowledge; and they would not give it up to any officer of the Central Government.

Ugartechea ordered a detachment of his troops to march upon Gonzales (76 miles), and take the gun by force. The colonists assembled to oppose him. Expresses were despatched to all parts of the country. The news flew with the speed of a race horse. The people rose in arms. They marched for the battlefield. OH, THE HEART-EACH OF SUSPENSE! — Before this time, in all human probability, the battle is won or lost — and we know not yet the result.

The Mexican despot, the letter says, rules a million of men — Texas has 7000 with American hearts and courage and determined to be free. The enemy have a well appointed cavalry, who are volunteers. The infantry is composed of convicts, who are placed in the army as a punishment for their crimes. Our riflemen are a deadly species of troops, as all the world knows, but in the prairies they will be powerless against cavalry. Bayonets and lances are what are, therefore, most needed by American volunteers.

MOBILE CHRONICAL

TEXAS VOLUNTEERS ..

Huntsville Alabama: Colonel Ponton S. Wyatt left this place on Sunday morning last, at the head of about thirty brave fellows, for Texas, who go to assist their brethern in that country in defending their rights, their families and homes, and their liberties against the Mexican usurper and his minions. They set out in the mist of a heavy rain — good omen of their willingness to bear the hardships and "endure to the end" — were escorted to the top of the hill by the "Huntsville Guards". The company and their commander — than no man stands higher in this community for honor, courage, or chivalry of feeling — carry with them the good wishes and applause of the best men among us. The company would, no doubt, have been much larger had time been allowed for recruiting. As Texas was actually invaded, Col. Wyatt thought it best to take up his line of march forthwith, hoping to gather recruits as he proceeded, under the impression that he carried with him about 50 extra stands of arms. The parting scene at Russell's Hill between the Volunteers and the Guards, and especially between the latter and their old commander (Col. Wyatt), was truly effecting. Success to their cause — success to the men — success to the flag which they will unfurl — the "stars and stripes!" — float where they will.

THE NEW YORK
MERCHANTILE ADVERTISER

VOLUNTEERS FOR TEXAS

We note that a vessel sails from this city today for Texas, with nearly two hundred volunteers. She goes direct to New Orleans, which port is to be the rendezvous for four other vessels also with volunteers — Immediately after their arrival they will leave in a body for Texas.

THE NEW YORK
COMMERCIAL ADVERTISER

IMPORTANT FROM MEXICO

The tidings of the recent movements in Texas had reached Mexico City, and as was expected, had produced a great excitement. The most energetic measures were resorted to without a moments delay, and there is every appearance that we shall soon hear of serious doings in the revolted province. A strong feeling of ill will and suspicion against the Americans resident in Mexico was aroused, and apprehensions were entertained of injury to their persons and property. A large number of commissions for privateers — the accounts say 500 — had been received at Vera Cruz, to be given out as occasion might require. The archbishop of Mexico and the bishop of Puebla, had undertaken to furnish the government with a million of dollars to carry on the war. (This is the most important movement of the whole, for the government is notoriously afflicted with extreme poverty.)

A division of 2000 infantry had been ordered to assemble at Matamoras, and 300 cavalry had begun their march to Texas. It is said that General Santa Anna himself would proceed thither to take the chief command.

The new constitution had been adopted by congress and proclaimed. Some opposition was made, but without effect.

TROY DAILY WHIG

FROM TEXAS

The troops from New Orleans, amounting to 500 men, had arrived at headquarters. A skirmish had taken place near Bexar, in which the Mexicans were repulsed with some loss and compelled to retire into the town. A gentleman who arrived at New Orleans from Nacogdochas, brought information that General Cos and all his forces had capitulated and surrendered themselves prisoners of war — being forced thereto by want of provisions in Bexar. This, however, is only rumor. In consequence of this the delegates to the general council, who had deferred assembling in order at attend to the more urgent business of fighting, were repairing to the appointed place of meeting.

The Texans appear to be confident and full of spirit and animation.

The following is the bulletin of the skirmish above referred to.

HEADQUARTERS,
MISSION OF CONCEPTION
(1½ miles from Bexar —
Oct. 28, 1835)

To the President of the Consultation of Texas.

I have the honor to inform you that the enemy, to the number of three hundred cavalry and one hundred infantry, as nearly as could be ascertained, with two pieces of artillery, at sunrise this morning attacked the detachment of the army under the command of Col. Bowie and Captain Fannin, composed of ninety men who were posted at this place, and after a warm engagement of three hours, were repelled with the loss of one piece of cannon, a six pounder, and about thirty muskets, and sixteen men left dead on the ground, and from all accounts as many more carried off; the wounded we can only conjecture, with the exception of two that remained on the field. It is with great regret I have to say that on our side we had one man, Richard Andrews, wounded, I fear mortally; but we have sustained no other loss except a few horses. The main body of the army came up about thirty minutes after the enemy had retired.

S. F. Austin

NEW ORLEANS BULLETIN

LATEST FROM TEXAS

"We are indebted to a friend, arrived last evening from Nacogdoches, for the following information from Texas. He informs us that Gen. Houston left San Felipe with a considerable reinforcement of troops, to join the Commander-in-Chief, Austin, near San Antonio. Our informant also states that he met a company of 80 men from the neighborhood of Nacogdoches; another of 33, and another of 25 from the same settlement; and the company of about 60 which went from this place, who were to be joined at Nacogdoches by an additional corps — all of whom were in high spirits and health, and marching on to San Antonio. A fine company of cavalry of 16 men, from the neighborhood of Natchez, were also met on their way. A letter was received from Labadie, stating that a Lieut. had captured a Mexican, from whom he learned that there was a reinforcement of Mexicans, of about 400, coming on to join Gen. Cos, whose army consisted of about 1700 men.

POSTSCRIPT —

A letter just received from Gen. Austin, informs us that a division of the army had advanced and taken up a position at Salada, within 5 miles of the city of San Antonio, in doing which they come in contact with the advance guard of the enemy, who still continued in sight of the hill between our troops and San Antonio. General Austin continues to urge reinforcement to hasten as fast as possible.

NEW ORLEANS UNION

SAN FELIPE DE AUSTIN:

Dear Sir — Knowing that your paper has a very extensive circulation in the United States, and believing that many of your readers feel a deep interest in the affairs of Texas at this time, I take the liberty of enclosing for your publication, a circular, containing extracts of letters from Gen. Austin, from which you will learn that we shall have something to do in reducing San Antonio. The forces of the enemy and that of the volunteers are about equal in number. Gen. Austin dispatched a communication to Gen. Cos, by a Mexican, stating, that he was supporting the principals of the Constitution of 1824, and inquiring how our flag would be received? His reply was, "disband your forces, return home peaceably, and then perhaps I will listen to your petitions, at present I can only regard you as rebels and traitors." We will teach him that we have rights independent of a dictator or military power, and that his haughty reply cannot influence Americans to compromise their rights.

Yours, Joseph Bryan

STILL LATER — We learn from a gentleman, that has just arrived, by land, from Texas, that the Texians had been able to surround Gen. Cos and his small army of 700 men, and that all chance of escape was shut out for him. The Texians speak confidently of an easy victory.

NEW YORK
COURIER AND INQUIRER

TEXAS . . .

Accounts from New Orleans announce the receipt there of a later intelligence from Texas. A provisional government had been completely organized, and a Bill of Rights adopted, which will be found below. Henry Smith appointed Governor, and J. W. Robinson, Lieutenant Governor. The Mexican General Cos, is completely surrounded at San Antonio by General Austin, with 2000 Texian forces. Five Texian vessels of war are scouring the whole of the Texian coast, and prevent the landing, by Mexican vessels, of any troops or supplies, while the passage is completely open for succours of all description to the Texians.

DECLARATION OF THE
PEOPLE OF TEXAS,
IN GENERAL
CONVENTION ASSEMBLED. —

Whereas, General Antonio Lopez de Santa Anna, and other military chieftans, have, by force of arms, overthrown the Federal Institutions of Mexico, and dissolved the social compact which existed between Texas and other Mexican Confederacy; now the good people of Texas, availing themselves of their natural rights, solemnly declare:

1st. That they have taken up arms in defence of their RIGHTS, and LIBERTIES which are threatened by the encroachments of military despots, and in defence of the Federal Constitution of Mexico, of 1824.

2nd. That Texas is no longer morally or civilly bound by the compact of union; yet, stimulated by the generosity and sympathy common to a free people, they offer their support and assistance to such of the members of the Mexican Confederacy as will take up arms against military despotism.

3rd. That they do not acknowledge that the present authorities of the nominal Mexican Republic have the right to govern within the limits of Texas.

4th. That they will not cease to carry on a war against the said authorities, whilst their troops are within the limits of Texas.

5th. That they will hold it to their right, during the disorganization of the Federal System, and the reign of despotism, to withdraw from the union, to establish an independent government, or to adopt such measures as they may deem best calculated to protect their rights and liberties; but that they will continue faithful to the Mexican Government, so long as that nation is governed by the Constitution and laws that were formed for the government of the Political Association.

6th. That Texas is responsible for the expenses of her armies, now in the field.

7th. That the public faith of Texas is pledged for the payment of any debts contracted by her agents.

8th. That she will reward by donations of land, all who volunteer their services in her present struggle, and receive them as citizens.

These declarations we solemn-

TEXAS . . .
(CONTINUED)

ly avow to the world, and call God to witness their truth and sincerity, and envoke defeat and disgrace upon our heads, should we prove guilty of duplicity.

B.T. Archer, President
P. B. Dexter, Secretary
Nov. 8, 1835

NEW ORLEANS BULLETIN

!! PARTICULARS OF THE CAPTURE OF GOLIAD !!

Dear Sir — While all eyes were directed with intense anxiety towards the military operations near Gonzales — supposing that to be the only point from whence we might expect important news — we were astonished at receiving information of the capture of Goliad, (La Bahia) by a party of colonists. These were volunteers from the transcendantly fertile banks of the Caney, and from the town of Matagorda, a place destined to become an important city.

Before the party entered the field, most of the volunteers were at Gonzales — and fearing that the harvest of honors would be reaped before they could arrive there — They struck off from La Baca with the daring determination of taking Goliad by surprise.

Goliad is situated on the southwest side of the San Antonio river, thirty leagues below Bexar, and it is fifteen leagues from Copono, the landing place of Aransas Bay, and about the same distance from La Baca, and of Matagorda Bay. The fort is built upon the point of a very steep and high hill, formed of rock, with a deep ravine upon one side and a low prairie extends towards the southwest.

The walls of the fort are of stone, and lime, and bear in places the marks of the storms of a hundred winters, but are still proof against anything less then the batterings of heavy artillery.

A long forced march brought the vanguard of the colonists to the San Antonio river, fording below the town at 11 o'clock on the night of the 9th inst. Here they halted for the main body, and to make arrangements for the attack.

A very small party was sent into the town, and they brought out a very worthy citizen, friendly to the constitution of 1824; and by his assistance guides were procured perfectly acquainted with the place.

The main body of the colonists missed their road in the night, and before they found out their mistake, were at the upper ford, immediately opposite the town. They then struck across for a shortcut, to the position occupied by the vanguard. Their route led through a mesquite thicket. While the parties were threading their way through this thicket, the horse of one of them started in fright at an object beneath a bush. The rider checked his horse and said, "who's there?" A voice answered in Spanish — One ognized the voice of an old acquaintance of La Bahia — and asked if it was not such a one, of the party supposed that he recmentioning the name — "No", was the reply, "My name is Milam."

Colonel Milam is a native of Kentucky. At the commencement of the Mexican War for Independence he engaged in the cause, and assisted in establishing the independence of the country. — When Iturbide assumed the purple, Milam's republican principals placed him in fetters — dragged him to the city of Mexico, and confined him in prison until the usurper was de-throned. When Santa Anna assumed the Dictatorship, the Republican Milam was again thrust into the prison at Monte Rey. But his past sufferings and services wrought upon the sympathies of his hard hearted jailors.

They allowed him the luxury of a bath. He profited by the in-

34

dulgence and made arrangements with an old compatriot to place a fast horse suitably equipped upon the bank of the stream at a time appointed. The Colonel passed the sentinel, as usual, — walked quietly on, — MOUNTED THE HORSE AND FLED!

Four hundred miles would bring him to safety. — The noble horse did his duty; and bore the Colonel clear of all pursuit to the place where our party surprised him. At first he supposed himself in the power of the enemy — but the ENGLISH LANGUAGE soon convinced him that he was in the mist of his own countrymen.

He had never heard that Texas was making an effort to save herself. No whisper of the kind had been allowed to pass his prison. When he learned the object of the party, his heart was full. He could not speak — FOR JOY!

When the company arrived at the lower ford they divided themselves into four parties of twelve men each. One party remained as a guard with the horses. The other three, each with a guide, marched by different routes to the assault.

Their axes hewed down the door where the colonel commanding the place was sleeping — and he was taken a prisoner from his bed. A sentinel hailed — and fired. A rifle ball laid him dead upon the spot. The discharge of firearms and the noise of human voices now became commingled. The Mexican soldiers fired from their quarters and the blaze of their guns served as targets for the colonist riflemen.

The garrison was called to surrender, and the call was translated by a gentleman present who spoke the language. They asked for terms.

The interpreter now became the chief speaker — "No," answered he. "They say they will massacre everyone of you, unless you come out immediately and surrender. Come out — come out quick. I cannot keep them back — come out if you wish to save your lives. I can keep them back no longer!" "Oh, do, for God's sake keep them back," answered the Mexicans in their own language — "We will come out and surrender immediately," — and they rushed out with all speed and laid down their arms.

And thus the fort of Goliad was taken. A fort which, with a garrison of three hundred and fifty patriots in the war of 1812-13, withstood a siege of an army of more than two thousand Spanish troops and forced them to retire — discomfitted.

At the capture of the fort three Mexican soldiers were killed and seven wounded, and one Colonel, one Captain, one Lieutenant with 21 petty officers and privates were made prisoners; others of the garrison escaped in the dark and fled.

In the fort were found two pieces of brass cannon, five hundred muskets and carbines, six hundred spears, along with ammunition and provisions.

One of the colonists was wounded in the shoulder.

Colonel Milam assisted in the capture of the fort and then spoke: "I assisted Mexico to gain her independence, I have spent more than twenty years of my life, I have endured heat and cold, hunger and hardship, I have borne losses and suffered prosecutions, I have been a tenant of every prison between this place and Mexico — but the events of this night have compensated me for all my losses and all my sufferings."

The colonists were commanded by George M. Collinsworth, but it would be difficult to find in the company a man not qualified for the command.

Goliad is of vastly more importance in a military point of view than Bexar, as the latter is in a valley upon the banks of a river commanded by the hills on both sides — therefore it is indefensible.

The main body of the army under Austin marched from Gonzales on the 13th inst. against Bexar.

When provoked, there is in Colonel Austin the courage of a lion; and there is in him, at all times, the caution of a fox. With him in command, if we do not wish for a speedy victory, we at least do not fear a defeat.

I send this by a soldier who fought at the capture of Goliad and if there be any error in my statements, you will have the means of correcting them before you.

THE NEW YORK COMMERCIAL ADVERTISER

TEXAS

If the accounts which reach us from Texas are correct the prospects of the Colonists in their contest against opposition, are every day brightening. The reported surrender of Cos to the Texians, we presume is premature, but admitting it to be so, still they have much to encourage them. The capture of Goliad, the defeat of the Mexicans in every skirmish which has hitherfore taken place, and the flocking in of auxiliaries from the United States, are among the encouraging circumstances which they have to acknowledge. The Macon (Georgia) Telegraph, states that 120 volunteers have gone from that place to Columbus; 500 are said to have gone from New Orleans — and from various other points of the South, North, and West, we hear of frequent departures for the "seat of war" — The New Orleans Bee brings information of the release of Governor Viesca, of Texas, who had been arrested and imprisoned by the order of the Mexican Government.

THE NEW YORK EVENING POST

FROM TEXAS

The steam packet Wm. Gibbions, arrived at N. Y. on Thursday morning last by which the Charleston papers, the Savannah papers, and the New Orleans papers have been received.

A meeting was held at Macon, Georgia, in behalf of the Texians, when the sum of $3,141 was subscribed on the spot — a committee appointed to solicit further donations — spirited resolutions were adopted, and TWENTY-NINE of the gentleman present immediately enrolled themselves as volunteers to march to the aid of their brethren in Texas. Amongst them, were Mr. Thomas W. Hazard, of S. Carolina, and Lieut. Hugh McLeoud,

recently from the Military Academy at West Point, who addressed the meeting in a spirit-stirring appeal, pledging himself to resign his commission and embark as a volunteer, in the cause of liberty; that the struggle in Texas needed SOLDIERS and not RESOLUTIONS; that we would tender them our persons and our arms on the contested field; that these would best express our sympathies in their behalf.

The Macon Messenger states, that these volunteers, and such others as might join them, were to be commanded by Colonel William Ward, and that they would take their departure for Texas soon.

THE NEW ORLEANS
TEXIAN AGENCY

LATEST FROM TEXAS

General Samuel Houston and Col. McComb have arrived from Texas. The latter brings intelligence that San Antonio has fallen; the Mexicans have been completely routed and driven across the river; that General Cos is beaten; and that the Texian army is almost daily augmented by volunteers

from various parts of the country.

We hope that this is more than a rumor: for, in giving publicity to many former statements, we found that we had been too credulous — our wish being for success on the part of our Texian friends. Yet still we wish victory ours.

NEW YORK
COURIER AND INQUIRER
!!LATE AND IMPORTANT FROM TEXAS!!

We received a letter, dated New Orleans, announcing that the town of San Antonio de Bexar has surrendered to the Texian forces, which at the last accounts were besieging it. General Cos, the Mexican commander, with a few of his troops had retired to the Alamo; but as the town was occupied by the Texians and their prisoners, and Cos' forces without provisions, he would be compelled to surrender himself a prisoner of war in a few days.

Thus has terminated, for months at least, the war in Texas, and no one who is familiar with her resources and the character of her people, can doubt her ability to establish her independence. That such may be the rich and merited reward of their patriotism is not only our earnest desire, but we most firmly believe, as we always have, that there is a spirit abroad in Texas, which can never be made to yield to the Despotic Government of Santa Anna. No other expedition can be fitted out by Mexico against Texas until spring; and then the army of the Patriots will be sufficiently strong to repel them.

In the meantime we learn by letters of our correspondents and the southern papers, that such is the confidence of our fellow citizens in the south in the justice of the Texian cause and the certainty of their success, that they are passing into the Territory by the thousands, as this is the land of promise. Full faith appears to be given Dr. Archer's declaration, "that Texas is the garden of the world."

"Colonel Travis Has Acted Nobly And Spiritedly."

PHASE #3

TEXIANS IN THE ALAMO EXPECT ATTACK . . . MEXICANS ADVANCE TO LARADO . . . UNHAPPY VOLUNTEERS LEAVE TEXAS . . . COLONEL TRAVIS AT THE ALAMO . . . MEXICAN TROOPS ADVANCING ON GOLIAD . . . THE SIEGE OF THE ALAMO . . . TEXIANS ARE REINFORCED BY 32 MEN FROM GONZALES . . . THE FALL OF THE ALAMO . . . DAVID CROCKETT NOT DEAD AS REPORTED . . . RETURN OF CROCKETT'S WATCH . . . COLONEL FANNIN UNDER SIEGE . . . REPORT OF FANNIN'S DEFEAT . . . FANNIN YET ALIVE . . . CONFIRMATION OF FANNIN'S DEATH.

THE NEW ORLEANS BEE

LATE AND IMPORTANT FROM TEXAS

We received intelligence yesterday from Texas, by which we learn that an express had been sent from Col. Neill, commanding at San Antonio, informing the provincial government that a force of 2500 men had been at Larado a short time before; and that 1500 of them had advanced as far as the Rio Frio, 80 miles distance from San Antonio. An attack on the latter place was daily expected. In the Alamo, a church-fortress, there was then only 75 men; with little provisions. The acting governor had issued a proclamation, calling on volunteers, to go to the defence of the Alamo.

(Once more into the breach, dear friend, once more, and let not Texas fall a prey to tyrants!!)

We also learn that the Texians were fitting out an army to seize Matamoras; and prove that they fight with Mexicans for the Constitution of 1824, and not against the Mexican Republic to which they have sworn allegiance under that Constitution.

They also resolved on another determination, which will meet with the approbation of our merchants who trade with Mexico — that is to desist from the contemplated system of privateering. We are requested, by competent authority to state this, in order to remove all the apprehensions of those engaged in the trade.

THE NEW ORLEANS TRUE AMERICAN

HIGHLY IMPORTANT FROM MEXICO ! !

By letters received from Vera Cruz, accounts from Santa Anna were, that he was waiting in San Louis, under the pretext of augmenting his force, to march against Texas, and they amounted to between 7 and 8 thousand men as reported, but that in fact, there was only between 2 and 3000, and although much was said about his campaign against Texas, he will not go there in person, fearing that there is a gathering storm at hand, and that he may be hustled from power; it is also stated that the Mexican Government views with distrust, all pledges on the part of the U.S., in preserving her neutrality.

By accounts from Campeachy, it appears that the report which has been circulated that there were vessels fitting out against Texas, is false. We also hear by accounts from Tampico and vicinity that the area was in a very great state of excitement against Santa Anna and his advisers; it is feared that another revolution is on the eve of breaking out, so much so that a body of 600 troops, ordered from Tampico to Texas, were detained, and more men were ordered from Mexico to co-operate with them in maintaining the present government. By private letters from Mexico, dissatisfaction throughout is very great against the despot, and that measures were taken in different states to overthrow his power by drawing him out of Mexico towards Texas. "God speed," that the despot may fall, and never raise his head again on the continent of America. That Santa Anna must fall is inevitable; we see through the mist, the dawn of light and liberty glimmering in every quarter, and that Mexico and Texas must be **free!**

THE NEW ORLEANS BEE

LATEST FROM TEXAS

An express from San Antonio de Bexar, arrived here yesterday, bringing dispatches from Lieut. Col. J. C. Neill, Commandant of that post. They convey to us the important information that the Mexicans had advanced as far as Larado and the Rio Frio river. Col. Neill has but 75 men with him in the Alamo. Under these circumstances they implore your aid in defending this important fortress against the common enemy. WILL YOU GO THERE??? I regret to make you at this season of the year, when the case of your domestic concerns, claims all your attention; but I am compelled to do it by the imminet danger which menaces your brothers in arms, by risks to which the inhabitants of our frontier will be exposed if we do not fly to their succor, and by the disgrace and ruin which the least delay will produce to our country.

Rally then my brave countrymen, under the standard of Constitutional Liberty; join together, and by your energy and valor, would be the saviours of a defenceless country. The preservation of your property requires it — your country, your families call you —

and who can remain deaf to their cries? Your lands — your dwellings are invaded — will you refuse to defend them? — The unprotected orphan makes to you a tacit but irresistible appeal; the infant, ignorant of the dangers which await it, your mothers, your sisters, your wifes, throw themselves in your arms, relying on your patriotism and indomitable valor. Fly then to the protection of your household goods; hasten to the west, where you will be organized for a short and glorious campaign. MARCH!! Victory awaits you; the Genius of Liberty has unfurled her banners and will crown her children with imperishable laurels. Carry back into the enemy's country all the horrors of war, and let the tyrant fall in a war of extermination. Since he will compel us to take up arms for our defence, let him see that Freemen know how to die as well as they know how to live!

March then without delay, and you will raise for yourselves an imperishable monument in the hearts of your fellow citizens. May the God of battles guide you to victory to honor, and to peace!

J. W. Robinson
Governor Ad Interim

BALTIMORE GAZETTE

NEWS FROM TEXAS

Volunteers are returning from Texas. As we heretofore predicted, they have found anything else there then food for frolic, and a report very discouragingly of the inhabitants of the country. In the camp, at San Antonio, the troops had been entirely out of bread stuff some days before our informant left, their food being Spanish beef. We wish not to cast a damp feeling upon the spirit of those disposed to see Texas free from the Mexican government, our own opinion being what it may. We are a friend to liberty anywhere and everywhere, in it's pure sense; but any information, whatever it may be, from Texas, we feel bound to give. Many that have returned from that country speak of the land as being rich and productive. But of its inhabitants they give a miserable account. They are said to be very poor, and care not a fig under what government they live. We speak of them generally; doubtless there are exceptions. The volunteers even have to pay for the food for their horses; they say there is no money there excepting what the volunteers take with them, and that the majority of the Texians that fight is plunder and pillage. The country is now free of Mexican troops, but Santa Anna is expected in the spring with a powerful force. The Texians are said to be indolent, and quite contented. The only lands that can be given to volunteers, are upon the head-waters of the streams, and back in the interior, the fine lands on the navigable streams being included in the grants to companies by the government. The weather during the winter has been a continual stream of sunshine, and no rains for two or three months.

THE NEW ORLEANS COURIER

LATEST FROM TEXAS

A gentleman has offered us a copy of the Red River Herald, containing the Declaration of Independence, made by the people in Texas in general convention. It is well written and will have a fine effect in uniting the people in resisting successfully, Santa Anna and his Myrmidoms!

THE NEW ORLEANS BEE

FROM TEXAS

"The intelligence of the repulse of the army of Santa Anna under Sesma and Cos by the garrison of Texians at the Alamo has been confirmed. — Colonel Travis has acted nobly and spiritedly; and there is no doubt that his example will be followed throughout Texas — in expelling the invaders. We have ourselves little hesitation in asserting that the continuance of the Mexican army in Texas will be very short lived, and we are aware of that blockade of the Texian ports is a mere gasconade. Capt. Hawkins, and the other officers of the Texian navy, will soon sweep the Gulf of all Mexican ships that dare to pass Matagorda."

NEW ORLEANS COMMERCIAL BULLETIN

LATE FROM TEXAS

Rumors from Texas say that Santa Anna has left the army, and is hastening back to the city of Mexico, in consequence of the death of Barragan, the acting President, by poison.

The whole Mexican force in Texas now is estimated at 5500 men. The right wing, composed of 700 men under the Mexican general Urrea, advancing by the Matamoras road upon Goliad, which was occupied by Col. Fannin with 500 Texians. The left wing of the Mexicans under Cos and Sesma, which advanced upon the Laredo road, was besieging the Alamo, at Bexar, and must probably soon obtain possession of the place, although it had been reinforced by 32 men from Gonzales. The whole number of Texians in the field to oppose Gens. Cos and Sesma, including volunteers and militia, is estimated at 1,500. It is conjectured that the Texians will retire before the Mexican force and concentrate their whole force so as to make battle in the woodland upon the banks of the Colorado; and this conjecture is founded upon the information received of a party of volunteers which were advancing to join Col. Fannin, having been ordered to halt at the Guadalupe, 25 miles in the rear of Col. Fannin's position. Col. Fannin, in whom is united science, and a thorough knowledge of military tactics — with unquestioned bravery — will be more than a match for Urrea — should the plan of the campaign render it necessary for him to give the latter battle. The great strength of the Texian forces consists in their riflemen; and these placed in the thickets upon the banks of the streams, will be more dangerous enemies than the Mexicans have ever yet met.

It is these which will render the country unconquerable!! Even if the Mexicans were to advance into the heart of the country, they must consider themselves as conquerors only of the country upon which their encampments are formed. They may here and there burn the humble log-cabin, and destroy the corn field of the poor settler, who has fled with his wife and children to the dense forest — where, if they pursue, they will find enemies who will deal with them death from every tree.

THE LOUISIANA ADVERTISER

EXTRA !!!!

THE FALL OF BEXAR !! THE ENTIRE OF THE TROOPS IN THE GARRISON PUT TO DEATH !! - COL'S CROCKETT AND BOWIE KILLED !!! -

The Southern mail has just arrived. The news from Texas is important. We have no room for particulars of the bloody battle in Texas except what is contained in the following:

The Alamo has fallen into the hands of the Mexicans under Santa Anna, and its garrison have been massacred in cold blood after their arms were surrendered, Col. David Crockett is among the slain.

We are indebted to a gentleman, a passenger on board the steamer Levant, from Nachitoches, for the annexed letter giving the particulars of the fall of the Alamo — it is a copy of one addressed to the editor of the Red River Herald:

"SIR: — Bexar has fallen! Its garrison was only 187 strong, commanded by Lieut. Col. Travis. After standing repeated attacks for two weeks, and an almost constant cannonade and bombarding during that time, the last attack was made on the morning of March 6th, by upwards of 2,000 men, under the command of Santa Anna in person; they carried the place about sunrise, with a loss of 520 killed, and about the same number wounded. After about an hours fighting the whole garrison was put to the sword, (save the sick and wounded and wounded and seven men who asked for quarter) — All fought desperately, until entirely cut down; the rest were murdered. The brave and gallent Travis, to prevent himself from falling into the hands of the enemy, shot himself. Not an individual escaped, and the news is known to us by a citizen of Bexar, who came to our army at Gonzales — but from the cessation of Travis' signal guns there is no doubt of its truth. The Declaration of Independence you have no doubt received, and you will, in a few days, receive the constitution proposed by the Republic.

Colonel's James Bowie and David Crockett are among the slain — the first was murdered in his bed, to which he had been confined by illness — the latter fell. fighting like a tiger. The Mexican army is estimated at 8,000 men; it may be more or less."

A. Briscoe

THE LOUISIANA ADVERTISER

FURTHER PARTICULARS OF THE
FALL OF THE ALAMO

We publish today further particulars of the FALL OF BEXAR, in Texas. The accounts are doubtless in the main correct, but coming to as they do, they must be received with some allowance. A strong sympathy already exists throughout the United States in favor of the Texian cause, particularly in the South, and the story of this bloody massacre will not be without its effect upon the public sentiment of this country. There is now every appearance that the struggle in Texas will be fierce and protracted. Having declared itself independent of Mexico, and established but recently a new State Government, there is every motive to urge them forward in the contest. — SANTA ANNA, on the other hand, in the true spirit of despotism, which has marked his whole career, is determined to compel his rebellious subjects to submit to his authority, or wage a war of extermination. May the cause of liberty prevail!

THE NEW ORLEANS TRUE AMERICAN

FURTHER NEWS ON THE FALL OF BEXAR

We learn by the passengers of the sch. Camanche, 8 days from Brazos River, that the war in Texas has at length assumed a serious character. Many of those who left this city, determined to lay down their lives in the cause of Texas, have bravely yielded them up at Bexar. Three young men from our office, we learn, are among the slain; the names of William Blazeby and Robert Moore have been mentioned to us; that of the other we could not ascertain.

On the 25th Feb. the Texian garrison in Bexar of 150 men only, commanded by Lieut. Col. W. B. Travis, was attacked by the advanced division of Santa Anna's army of about 2,000 men, when the enemy were repulsed with the loss of many killed and wounded, variously estimated from 450 to 600 without a loss of a single man of the garrison.

This great slaughter was ascribed to the fact that every man of the garrison had about eight guns loaded by his side.

Between the 25th of Feb. and the 2nd March, the Mexicans were employed in forming entrenchments around the Alamo and bombarding the place. On the 2nd March Col. Travis wrote that 200 shells had been thrown into the Alamo without injuring a man.

On the 1st of March, 32 men from Gonzales made their entry through the enemy's lines and reached the Alamo, making the whole number in the garrison 182.

On the 6th March, about midnight, the Alamo was assaulted by the entire force of the Mexican army, commanded by Santa Anna in person. The Mexicans fought desperately until daylight, when seven only of the garrison were found alive. We regret to say that Col. David Crockett and his companion Mr. Benton, also the Col. Bonham of South Carolina, were of the number who cried for quarter but were told there was no mercy for them. They then continued fighting until the whole were butchered. One woman (Mrs. Dickinson) and a wounded negro servant of Col. Travis were the persons in the Alamo whose lives were spared. Gen. Bowie was murdered in his bed, sick and helpless. Gen. Cos on entering the fort ordered Col. Travis's servant to point out to him the body of his master; he did so, when Cos drew his sword and mangled his face and limbs with the malignant feeling of a savage.

The bodies of the slain were thrown into a heap in the center of the Alamo and burned. On Gen. Bowie's body being brought out, Gen. Cos said that he was too brave a man to be burned like a dog — then added, PEW NO ES COSO ESCHADE — never mind, throw him in. The loss of the Mexicans in storming the place was estimated at not less than 1,000 killed and mortally wounded, and as many more disabled — making with their loss in the first assault, between 2,000 and 3,000 killed and wounded. It is worthy of remark that the flag of Santa Anna's army at Bexar was a BLOOD RED ONE, in place of the constitutional tri-colored flag.

49

FURTHER NEWS ON THE FALL OF BEXAR
(CONTINUED)

Immediately after the capture of the place, Gen. Santa Anna sent Mrs. Dickinson and Col. Travis, servant to Gen. Houston's camp, accompanied by a Mexican with a flag, who was bearer of a note from Santa Anna, offering the Texians peace and a general amnesty, if they would lay down their arms and submit to his government. Gen. Houston's reply was, "True, sir, you have succeeded in killing some of our brave men, but the Texians are not yet whipped." The effect of the fall of Bexar throughout Texas was electric. Every man who could use a rifle, and was in a condition to take the field, marched forthwith to the scene of war. It was believed that not less of 4,000 riflemen were on their way to the army when the Comanche sailed, to wreak their vengance on the Mexicans, and determined to grant no quarter.

Gen. Houston had burnt Gonzales, and fallen back on the Colorado with about 1,000 men.

Col. Fannin was in the fort at Goliad, a very strong position, well supplied with munitions and provisions, and from 400 to 500 men.

The general determination of the people of Texas seemed to be to abandon all the occupations and pursuits of peace, and continue in arms until every Mexican east of the Rio del Norte should be exterminated.

About the same time Col. Johnson, while reconnoitering to the westward of San Patricio, with a party of 70 men, were surrounded in the night by a large body of Mexican troops. In the morning the commander sent a summons to surrender at discretion, which was refused, and an offer to surrender as prisoners of war made. This was acceded to by the Mexican officer, but no sooner had the Texians marched out of their encampment and stacked their arms than a general fire was opened upon them by the whole Mexican force, when the prisoners attempted to escape — only three effected it, among them Col. Johnson and one man that had been wounded.

THE LOUISVILLE JOURNAL

CONVICTS USED TO STORM BEXAR ! ! !

A very intelligent gentleman, just arrived from Texas, has given us an interesting account of the manner in which Santa Anna stormed the fortress of the Alamo. The tyrant brought with him 1,508 convicts from the Mexican prisons. On arriving at San Antonio, he placed the whole body of them as a forelorn hope in advance of the rest of the army half encompassing them in the rear of 3,300 infantry, and placing still further in the rear 2,200 cavalry with orders that each convict who attempted to escape or retreat, should be instantly shot or cut down. He then ordered the convicts to storm the fortress, setting before them liberty and promotion if they succeeded, and immediate death in the event of their failure. They rushed forward with the fury of devils, and, in less than an hour, every man in the garrison was massacred. Out of the fifteen hundred, all but three or four hundred were either killed or mortally wounded.

THE CINCINATTI WHIG

LATE AND IMPORTANT!
COLONEL DAVID CROCKETT NOT DEAD!

We are much gratified in being able to inform our readers that COLONEL CROCKETT, the hero and patriot, it is said, IS NOT DEAD!! The cheering news is brought by a gentleman now in this city, directly from Texas, and who left the Colonel, as he states, three weeks ago, at the house of his brother-in-law in Texas, where the Colonel was lying quite ill, but gradually though slowly recovering from his wounds.

The gentleman who brings this news is known to a number of our citizens, who believe him to be a man of veracity. He states that Crockett was left upon the battle-ground of the Alamo covered with wounds, and, as the Mexicans supposed, - dead. That after the Mexicans had abandoned the place, Crockett was discovered by some of his acquaintances to be lying among the slain, still exhibiting signs of life. He was immediately taken care of, and conveyed to comfortable lodgings, as before stated, where his wounds were dressed, and every attention necessary to his recovery paid him. He had received a gash with a tomahawk on the upper part of the forearm, a ball in his left arm, and another one through his thighs, besides several other minor wounds. When the gentleman left his brother-in-law's house, Crockett was doing well.

Candor compels us to say that there are many improbabilities in relation to the truth of this report, but the respectable character of the gentleman who says he saw him with his own eyes in the condition and under the circumstances above stated, induces us to give it credit. We have, nevertheless, some doubts of its truth. We give the story, however, as the gentleman represented it, and we sincerely hope that it may prove entirely authentic. It is either true, or the man who has detailed to numerous persons in the city the above statements, is a LYING VILLIAN! It is due him to say, however, that those persons here that know him, give entire credit to his statements.

JACKSON TENNESSEE
TRUTH TELLER

A LETTER TO MRS. DAVID CROCKETT

Lost Prairie, Ark. 1836
Mrs. David Crockett,

Dear Madam. — Permit me to introduce myself to you as one of the acquaintances of your much respected husband, Col. Crockett. Of his fate in the fortress of the Alamo, in Texas, you doubtless are long since advised. With sincere feelings of sympathy, I regret his untimely loss to your family and self. For if among strangers, he constituted the most agreeable companion, he doubtless, to his beloved wife and children, must have been a favorite peculiarly prized. In his loss, Freedom has been deprived of one of her bravest sons, in whose bosom universal philanthrophy glowed with a genial warmth as ever amimated the heart of an American citizen. When he fell, a soldier died. To bemoan his fate, is to pay a tribute of grateful respect to Nature — he seemed to be her son.

The object of this letter is to beg you to accept the watch which accompanies it. You will doubtless know it when you see it. And as it has his name engraved on its surface, it will no doubt be the more acceptable to you.

As it will probably be gratifying to you to learn in what way I became possessed of it, permit me to state, that, last winter (the precise date not recollected by me), Col. Crockett, in company with several other gentlemen, passed through Lost Prairie, on the Red River, (where I live). The company, except the Colonel, who was a little behind, road up to my house and asked for accommodations for the night. My family being so situated, from the indisposition of my wife, that I could not accommodate them, they got quarters at one of my neighbors' houses. The Colonel visited me the next day and spent the day with me. He observed, whilst there, that his funds were getting short and as a means of recruiting them, he must sell something. He proposed to me to exchange watches — he priced his at 30 dollars more than mine, which sum I paid him, and we accordingly exchanged.

With his open frankness, his natural honesty of expression, his perfect want of concealment, I could not but be very much pleased. And with the hope that it might be an accommodation to him, I was gratified at the exchange, as it gave me a keepsake which often reminds me of an honest man, a good citizen and a pioneer in the cause of liberty, amongst his suffering brethren in Texas.

His military career was short. But though I deeply lament his death, I cannot restrain my American smile at the recollection of the fact that he died as a United States soldier should die, covered with his slain enemy, and even in death presenting to them his clenched fists, the weapons of their destruction.

We hope the day is not too far distant, when his adopted land will be freed from a savage enemy, and afford to yourself and children, a home rendered in every way comfortable, by the liberal donations of her government.

Accept, dear madam, for yourself and family, the most sincere wishes for your future.

Your most obt. servant:
Isaac N. Jones

(Editor's note: The following account has been included into the text as a side-light feature in order that the reader may have a short history in regards to the Bowie knife and of it's fate after the fall of the Alamo.)

THE PENNSYLVANIAN

(JULY 19, 1838)
THE BOWIE KNIFE

The papers the other day had a great deal of twaddle about the origin of the Bowie Knife; their statements were entirely wrong! The first person who had a Bowie knife in this country, was the father of Col. James Bowie, who was killed in the Alamo. The old man was originally from Scotland, and settled a plantation up the Red River. He used it altogether as a hunting and a cane knife. Col. James Bowie, or as he was more familiarly called Jim Bowie, **improved** upon it, as he thought, and first used the weapon in a duel. He became notorious by his bloody duel at Iberville, on the Plaquemine Bayou, in Louisiana; he was there shot down, and his antagonist was stooping over him to despatch him, Jim Bowie seized him by the waist, and cut him nearly in half with his knife. The "brother" of Jim Bowie, spoken in the Express as the inventor, is Rezin Bowie, who lately lived at Thibadouxville, on the Bayou La Fourcha, near Lake Chicot, in Louisiana. He is nearly blind; and so far from being what he is described in the Express, used to be a perfect rowdy, as was Jim Bowie himself. Again the Express says that Jim Bowie used the knife at the Alamo. This is untrue; he was sick and helpless, and was butchered in bed. Col. Almonte told the writer of this article so; and Jim Bowie informed us of the history and origin of the knife as described above. This was also corroberated by Dr. Grant, of Nova Iberia, Attakapas, in whose possession he saw the original knife in 1836. The knife found with Colonel Bowie's baggage in the Alamo, is now in the possession of Miss Charlotte Cushman, of the Park Theatre, New York.

54

SANTA ANNA AND HIS STAFF ON THE DAY BEFORE THE ASSAULT AND CAPTURE OF THE ALAMO. MARCH 6, 1836.

The scene represents a consultation held by Santa Anna and his principal staff officers outside of his headquarters in Bejar, at which a majority of them disagreed with his decision to mount the attack without delay, but Santa Anna's opinion prevailed.

In the foreground, from left to right, are shown:

RAMON MARTINEZ CARO, Santa Anna's civilian private secretary who accompanied him throughout the Texas campaign and was captured at San Jacinto. He is shown at his field desk, writing down the minutes of the discussion.

A STAFF TRUMPETER of the light cavalry, who always accompanied Santa Anna, to transmit orders and signals.

COLONEL FRANCISCO DUQUE, back turned, who lead the 2nd. assault column and who fell in the attack.

SANTA ANNA stands in the center of the group in undress uniform, with the blue sash of a division General. Behind his right shoulder, **GENERAL MARTIN PERFECTO COS,** in cavalry dress, who lead the 1st. column. Behind his left shoulder, **COLONEL JUAN MORALES,** who lead the 4th. column.

LT. COLONEL AGUSTIN AMAT, Santa Anna's second in command, and commanding officer of the Sapper Battalion, in shako and uniform with crimson facings of the Army Engineers.

GENERAL JOAQUIN RAMIREZ Y SESMA, last on the right, and commanding the Cavalry units.

In the middle ground, from l. to r.: A sgt. of the Sapper Battalion, back turned; a private of the regular Matamoros Battalion, in Shako; a private of the Jimenez Battalion, in barracks cap; a private of the Aldama Battalion rifle company, with green facings. All wear the regulation dark uniform decreed in June 1833. On the ground is a stack of ladders prepared for scaling the Alamo walls. Behind them the tents of the troop encampment, and beyond, a trench dug as the assembly point for the columns before going over the top, meantime occupied by sentries.

In the background is the west wall of the Alamo, surrounded by the grass-rimmed irrigation ditch that ran all around the compound. The northern battery is set at the left corner, behind the pecan tree; the 18 pound gun is at the right. Protruding above the wall in the center is the two story hospital building with an unfinished tower on which the Alamo battle flag was hoisted, and the front of the half-demolished church.

55

SANTA ANNA AND HIS STAFF ON THE DAY BEFORE THE
ASSAULT AND CAPTURE OF THE ALAMO: MARCH 6, 1836

56

THE ALAMO: 5 A.M.

EXPLANATORY NOTES TO THE "ALAMO" SCENES.

THE ALAMO - 5 A.M.

This composition is based on recent documentary research and re-appraisal of the assault on the Alamo. Previous representations in paintings, drawings, motion pictures and television pieces, some of them of considerable merit, perpetuate a few persistent errors which our color drawing has tried to correct.

Practically all previous representations show the assault taking place in broad daylight. Actually, the assault was undertaken under cover of complete darkness, before dawn on a March night. When a sullen sun broke through about 7:30 AM, the battle was over, and by 8 AM Santa Anna was already dictating his victory report. Another popular inaccuracy likes to represent the main assault, defense and battle taking place in front and inside the picturesque Alamo church. The disposition of Mexican troops, the assault order and subsequent battle reports indicate that the Church and palisade at the south-east corner of the Alamo compound were not attacked frontally from the outside. No attack column had been assigned to this conspicuous corner. The four attack columns were thrown against the north-west, north-east, east and south-west walls. After the attackers broke into the compound, the defenders fell back toward the south-east corner and the Church, where they made their last stand against the attackers who were closing in from the inside of the compound, not from the outside.

Our composition shows the beginning of this operation, shortly after 5 AM. Far in the left background, Santa Anna with his staff and his reserve of Grenadier, Rifle and Sapper companies standing at the Mexican North Battery, supervises the attack. The 1st assault column under Gen. Cos, made a run against the NW corner, was badly mauled by cannon and rifle fire, fell back and is now being led in a circular detour against the West enclosure. The 2nd column, under Col. Duque, bears against the NE corner and the battery where Travis stood. The 3rd column, Col. Romero, is moving up against the East wall defended by riflemen only. The 4th column, under Morales, is forcing the heavily defended SW corner, between the San Antonio river and the 3-cannon earthwork and ditch protecting the main gate. No column operated against the Churchyard palisade, allegedly defending by Crockett and the Tennessee Volunteers.

It has become customary to show the Mexican troops piling into the churchyard from the outside in a disorderly mob, wearing a variety of blue, white, red and nondescript uniforms, waving a multitude of national flags and the top of their shakos painted as a tricolor bullseye, all of this erroneous interpretation of the plates in Linati's 1820 lithographs. In reality, the units assigned to the assault, were picked companies, the best Santa Anna had at hand on that day, disciplined and trained veterans, survivors of the murderous forced marches from San Luis to Texas. They attacked in closed company columns, led by their officers and flanked by their buglers and drummers. They did not wear multicolored uniforms, least of all the white ones as used in the tropical hot country. The standard uniform was then dark blue with red facings and yellow unit identification on the collar. No flags were carried by the attack columns; only the Sapper Battalion might have had its "colonel's flag" with it, and it was

58

this flag that was hoisted over the Alamo after the Texan colors were hauled down. Our scene shows the three Texan flags that were present at the Alamo and were most likely flying from the walls as shown: Over the main gate, the tricolor with the Texas-Coahuila stars and the date 1824 on the reverse, which the colonists brought with them when they left Bejar to occupy the Alamo; over the tallest or Hospital building, the **real** Alamo Battle Flag which Travis brought with him when he took command and to which he referred in his Letter to All Americans; and the New Orleans Company guidon over the infantry quarters. The layout of the compound itself, follows the latest available information obtained by several good researchers and specialists in recent times. Actually, the grounds around the Alamo should appear much darker, as it was still night when the assault got under way; but this would have made the scene too dark to distinguish the approaches and the assault columns; hence the lighter tone of the background. The inside of the Alamo, as confirmed by Santa Anna in his report, was lit up brightly by incessant artillery and musketry fire of the defenders, and the bursting projectiles.

Although there is never a "last word" in history, and much more accurate information about the fall of the Alamo may still turn up as time goes by, I believe that the details of this scene come as close to the real action as was humanly possible to imagine and reconstruct. Anybody with enough patience could count the small figures of the defenders and verify that they are 184, omitting Col. Bowie who was ill indoors.

THE ALAMO - 8 A.M.

I believe this is the first time anybody endeavored to reconstruct, guided by serious documentation, the dramatic moment when Santa Anna came face to face with the last fallen defenders of the Alamo, among them David Crockett.

Wearing his Division General's full dress, accompanied by Cols. Romero and Morales, surrounded by his reserve troops and elated by his complete victory, Santa Anna is issuing his last orders. Crockett's body is not shown in the popularly accepted hunter's dress, as eye-witness reports state that he wore city clothes and a wide overcoat with cape. Corpses of defenders and attackers strew the ground. The Mexican uniforms, from left to right, are those of the Sappers (dark blue, black facings, dark red piping, brush pompon on shako), the Riflemen (dark blue, red facings and green pompon), the regular Matamoros Battalion officer (dark blue coat, light blue trousers, red facings and conical pompon). Coming through the gate in the background are a subaltern and privates of the Jimenez fusiliers, who had hauled down the Alamo Battle Flag described in a note by Crockett, and in a Mexican government circular. The southern column of the Church gate is visible at right, with smoke issuing from the interior where a 3-cannon battery and the powder room had been.

Santa Anna did not, as is sometimes shown, take part personally in the attack, leading troops. He rode down from his observation post after the fort had fallen and the sun had come up, entered by the gate, dismounted and walked over to the church yard, to convince himself that all resistance had collapsed and all the defenders were dead.

59

THE ALAMO: 8 A.M.

SAN JACINTO - 21 APRIL 1836 - 4:15 P.M. - CAPTURE OF THE 12 POUNDER

61

SAN JACINTO - 21 APRIL 1836 - 4:15 P.M.

CAPTURE OF THE 12-POUNDER.

Close-up view of a decisive moment of the battle, when Texans broke through the Mexican breastworks, cutting off and capturing the larger Mexican field piece, finishing off the gun crew and shooting down General Castrillon who in vain tried to rally the remnants of the troops. This scene is looking from North-West to South-East of the battle area. The far right background shows the fringe of the woods with the forward tents of the Mexican camp and reserve line, while the water of the San Jacinto River in the far left background glistens in the late afternoon sun.

According to Santa Anna's report and manifesto, recorded in Gen. Filisola's "Memories", 3 companies of infantry covered the woods; the regular Matamoros Battalion and the gun stood in the center; one infantry company, another gun and the cavalry formed the left of the advance post. At the moment of surprise, one column of Texans overran the three companies and occupied the woods; another Texan foot column attacked the center, while the left wing was being pierced by Texans on foot and on horse. The Mexican veteran units stood their ground and were wiped out, but the bulk of the Mexican line and reserves, consisting of ill-trained recent recruits, turned and fled in the only way open to them, toward the swampy banks of the San Jacinto River. This in brief is the situation shown in the painting: the Texans breaking through from the right, left and center; the confusion of the Mexicans who were just then doing camp fatigue duties, cleaning guns, watering horses and preparing their evening meal. In spite of the general panic, the gunners managed to fire off three rounds from "The Golden Standard" before the attackers were upon them. Smoke from the last shot is still drifting from the barrel. The bulk of the raw troops are in full flight toward the swampy river bank. The close-up permitted to suggest some of the despair, surprise and choas among the defenders, as well as the rage, drive and individual initiative of Houston's ragged fighters.

The representation of weapons, uniforms and dress on both sides conforms as much as possible, to objects in use at that time, as were also the facial features. On the Mexican side are shown the artillerymen defending the gun, soldiers of the regular Matamoros Battalion manning the breastwork, General Castrillon in field dress, and beside him some soldiers of the Toluca Active Militias.

It is our hope, in this modest way, to bring to life again and to conserve the memory of one of the crucial moments of this decisive action.

62

THE NEW YORK STAR

LATEST FROM TEXAS !!!

Letters from Texas state: "In my next, I shall have the pleasure of advising you of the extermination of Santa Anna's Army."

The rumor of the day is, that he offered to capitulate, and let us alone in the future, if a safe conduct for himself and his army, to the west of the Rio Grande be conceded to him. NOT GRANTED.

Further advices from the same place state that the city of New Orleans has the appearance of a military barracks; that the citizens are excited to the highest degree, and that they are determined to aid their struggling friends to the utmost extent against a foe, who have, by their savage barbarity, and violated faith to prisoners of war, excluded themselves from the privilages granted to civilized nations.

Advices state — "The current of emigration to Texas is beyond all former precedent; not less than 70 men daily pass here for Texas, during the week."

The rumor stated in the above extract of a letter from New Orleans, is no doubt correct. Col. Fannin with 500 men was at the fort at Goliad, and a detachment of about 1,000 men, of Santa Anna's army, has besieged him there. The volunteers from Matagorda, would march directly to that point and by a simultaneous sortie from that fort, and attack from the volunteers in the rear of the detachment, it was expected the army could be routed, and that Col. Fannin could then march with an increased force, and fall upon the rear of Santa Anna's main army, near San Antonio.

In confirmation of the above important rumor, the Mobile Chronical contains a letter from W. C. White & Co., dated at Columbia, (60 miles below San Felipe, about the same distance from Bexar) which states that the loss of the Mexicans in the massacre of the Alamo was over 2,000 killed and wounded. That an attack was intended by Santa Anna, upon Goliad, which was garrisoned by 650 Texians, under Col. Fannin. The letter adds that a decided battle would be fought on or near the Colorado river, to which place the headquarters of the army had removed, and where Gen. Houston commanded in person. There were 1,500 Texians in the field, and the numbers hourly increasing.

BALTIMORE GAZETTE

TEXAS

An extract of a letter received by a gentleman in this city, from J. Cable, of Natchitoches, dated 30th March, 1936:

The Texians have had a number of fights lately, this side of San Antonio, and I believe have been victorious. There are so many flying reports, that few are credited.

J. Cable, esq.

TROY DAILY WHIG

TEXAS

The rumor that has been current in the city for a couple of days, was confirmed by the arrival last evening of the schooner Equity from Brazoria. Capt. Martin, of that schooner, states that Fannin, preferring to join the Texian army, then concentrating on the Colorada River, had blown up the Fort of Goliad, where he was garrisoned, and completely demolished the town. With 500 troops under his command, he then cut his way through the Mexican army, encamped in the neighborhood, and effected a junction with the Texians under Gen. Houston. A decisive action was daily expected between Santa Anna and Houston. The Mexican army amounts to nearly 5,000 men, infantry, and cavalry; the Texians to about 2,500, more determined than well equipt.

Santa Anna has prosecuted his intention of exterminating the Texians. Agreeably to his positive and personal orders none are exempted from slaughter, of any age or sex over ten years. Several women and children have therefore been brought hither in the schooner Equity as a refuge from destruction. — All the Texians capable of bearing arms have volunteered or been summoned to the conflict; but as Houston and his forces are anxious for vengeance as well as victory; he has resolved, to bring the war to a speedy issue, and expel the invaders from the country.

Previous to blowing up the fort at Goliad, the Georgia volunteers consisting of 150 men under Colonel Ward attacked a body of 600 Mexicans at Refugio, 250 of whom are reported to have been killed and the rest routed. It is also stated that Gen. Houston attacked the advance guard of the Mexican army, which was repelled on the main body; and some prisoners were taken, among whom were two spies of the enemy.

It is also stated that the Brig Privilege which sailed hence with provisions for the Mexican army, had been captured by the Texian cutters.

It had been rumored that the Mexicans had captured Matagorda, but this is doubted.

It may well be that our citizens should reflect that the relation of this country has been altered by the late declaration of Independence by the Texians. — Previous to that, doubts might reasonably have been entertained of the propriety of interfering, in consequence of the alliance treaties between the United States and Mexico. This position has been totally altered by Texas being declared free and sovereign: so that Texas is now placed in the same position with regard to the American Union, as the Confederacy of the Thirteen United Colonies was with regard to the nations of Europe, after our declaration of independence was proclaimed. Before that event, the continental nations of Europe doubted the propriety of interference, in consequence of their treaties with England; but after that, France and Spain willingly and openly contenanced and supported our revolutionary struggles. The United States dissolving their connection with Great Britain, became a sovereign nation; so that Texas having dissolved her connection with Mexico, has become a distinct

65

nation. Any support consequently given to Texas, cannot be considered as given against Mexico, according to the international law — Texas being no longer an intergral part of the Mexican empire.

If we were anxious that our revolutionary struggles should be supported as well as contenanced by France and Spain, shall we fail in conceding that support to Texas which we desired and required when placed in similar circumstances?

TROY DAILY WHIG

LATE AND IMPORTANT FROM TEXAS

Intelligence has been received in New York by way of Mobile, announcing the defeat of Colonel Fannin and the capture of San Felipe by the Mexicans under General Santa Anna. General Houston had retreated to the east side of the Brazos. It is reported that Colonel Fannin had been killed and his army annihilated. — The inhabitants were moving in great haste to the Sabine. The Texans burnt San Felipe before they abandoned it.

Santa Anna's army was advancing upon the Brazos, in two divisions, one upon the coast and the other in the interior. It was the intention of the Texans to destroy all their towns, rather than suffer them to fall into the hands of the Mexicans.

All the country west of the Brazos has been abandoned. Reinforcements are arriving daily to join the army under General Sam Houston.

THE NEW ORLEANS TRUE AMERICAN

LATE NEWS FROM TEXAS -

We are overwhelmed this morning, with a huge mass of rumors, letters, and paragraphs, some accordant and some contradictory, and from among which we find it difficult to make up anything like an orderly or connected statement. Nevertheless we must attempt it, inasmuch as we have little room for extracts.

First, then of Col. Fannin and his little band. — The latest account is the following;

When Colonel Fannin commenced his march from Goliad, (having previously received orders from General Houston to join him with his men) he advanced into a large prairie, at some distance from that place, and was soon aware that the enemy had knowledge of his movements by preceiving that a large body of them had nearly surrounded him. On being thus apprised of his situation, he despatched three men to his advance guard, which were at a distance of seven miles, to aquaint them with his position, and advising them not to return. An engagement soon after commanced, and continued for three hours, when night put a stop to the contest. Fannin fell back on a small creek and entrenched himself.

The next morning the Mexicans hoisted a white flag upon which Fannin met him half way, when their commander expostulated with him, saying that further resistance on his part would be useless, adding that he had him entirely in his power, and at the same time offering terms of capitulation: First that they were to lay down their arms and wait until an exchange of prisoners could be made; secondly, that they should make an oath not again to take up arms against the Mexicans; and that a passage would be provided for them in ten days for New Orleans. The latter proposal Fannin and his men accepted. They were accordingly detained eight days of the time agreed on, when they were marched out in file (guarded on both sides by the Mexicans) as they supposed, to some port, preparatory to embarkation for this city. They had not however, proceeded above five miles, when the troops from one side cautiously fell back until they had them directly in front, when they, with those remaining on the other side, commenced an unexpected fire upon the prisoners. Four of Fannin's force which consisted of 388 men, exclusive of the advance guard, attempted an escape, but only one of the number effected it, from whom we received this intelligence. He succeeded in evading their search by concealing himself in a thicket, from whence he could preceive the enemy all around, like bloodhounds ready to pounce on their prey. His safety in such a critical position may well be attributed to a special interposition of Providence.

ALBANY ARGUS

TEXAS

By the official despatch of Jose Urrea, the Mexican General, to whom Colonel Fannin capitulated, which we find copied from the Mercurio of Matamoras, it would seem that Colonel Fannin, and his troops are still alive, prisoners of war. General Urrea says that, "The fortress of Goliad remains at the disposition of the supreme government. So are likewise their leader, Fannin, and more than 300 soldiers," etc. And in another despatch, — "I have in my power more than 600 prisoners, who I intend shall rebuild the houses they burnt at Goliad."

TROY DAILY WHIG

FROM TEXAS

The intelligence from Texas continues to be very contradictory, and the accounts received usually contain so exaggerated a description of the situation of affairs in that country, that it is exceedingly difficult to tell what the truth of the matter really is.

The latest accounts from New Orleans to us, state that Gen. Houston had retreated 28 miles from the Colorado, the enemy having advanced to the opposite shore.

An article from the New Orleans Bee states that Colonel Fannin had destroyed the fort at Goliad — burnt the town, and attempted to cut his way through the Mexican army, and that he was surrounded by the Mexicans and was compelled to capitulate, after which he and all his men were shot.

Much of the intelligence from Texas rests upon rumor.

THE PENSACOLA GAZETTE

!GLORIOUS NEWS!   !COLONEL FANNIN YET ALIVE!

Captain Tresuvan, of the Texian army, passed through this place on his way from Texas to South Carolina. Capt. T. was with Fannin when he was captured, and was one of the only three or four that escaped that massacre. He gives some particulars connected with this melancholy and disgraceful tragedy, which we had not heard before. It seems the Texican prisoners were marched out and formed in a line before they had any intimation of the fate that awaited them.

After they had been disposed in the manner best suited to the object which the Mexican commander had in view, that officer, with much apparent emotion, announced to the prisoners that it was his painful duty to have them all shot, and recommended to them to make their peace with heaven. A few only survived the fire of the Mexicans, and among them was our informant, who contrived, under the cover of smoke, to break through the Mexican outposts and make his escape. In the company with a Kentuckian, whose name is not given, he wandered through the woods for several days, and at length reached the army of General Houston. Capt. T., STATES POSITIVELY THAT COL. FANNIN WAS NOT AMONG THE SLAIN, BUT WAS PRESERVED AND IS STILL A PRISONER WITH THE MEXICANS!!

THE ALBANY EVENING JOURNAL

!!CONFIRMATION OF THE MURDER OF COLONEL FANNIN AND HIS SOLDIERS!!

Some of our editorial brethren, we are afraid, are rather vain in their political skepticism. There are those among them who still discredit the massacre of Col. Fannin's troops. For the benefit of such, we record another minuet evidence, — a letter written by one of the few who escaped, to his father. —

"Dear Father, — I take this opportunity of writing you a few lines to let you know that I am still in existence. I suppose you will have heard before this reaches you, that I was either taken prisoner or killed. I was taken prisoner on the 20th of last month, and kept a week, when all of us who were taken with Col. Fannin, besides other prisoners, were ordered out to be shot, but I with six others, out of five hundred and twenty-one escaped. Before we were taken, Col. Fannin's party had a battle with the Mexicans in a large prairie, and killed and wounded, as the Mexicans themselves said, three hundred of them; but one of the Texians, who was a prisoner at the time, says that it took them all the night of the 19th to bury their dead, and that we must have killed and wounded something like 800 or 1,000. Their force was 1,900 — ours 250.

"The circumstances under which we were taken are these: We were completely surrounded, without any provisions or water and in such a situation that we could not use our cannon; in consequence of which we thought it best to surrender on the terms offered to us — which were to treat us as prisoners of war, and according to the rules of christian warfare. But how sadly we were deceived the sequel will show; after starving us a week they ordered us out, saying we were going after beef, but when we had marched about half a mile from the fort we were ordered to halt. The Mexicans marched all on one side of us, and took deliberate aim at us, but I, as you have seen, was fortunate enough to escape. I have, however, had monstrous hard times, having nothing to eat for five successive days and nights, but at length arrived safely here this morning, after a travel of two weeks through prairies and dangers, during which time I had some narrow escapes, especially the night before last on the line of the picket guards of the Mexican force, I was near being killed or taken.

"San Felipe is taken. The Mexicans are in Texas, but I think I shall live to see her free notwithstanding. We have near 1,500 men in camp, and expect to attack the enemy in a few days.

"I am well with the exception of very sore feet occasioned by walking through the prairies barefooted. Tomorrow I shall go over the river to a farm to stay until I get entirely well, when I will try to avenge the death of some of my brave friends. — All my company were killed.

"Your affectionate son,
"CHAS. B. SHAIN."

THE NEW YORK STAR

THE MASSACRE OF FANNIN'S COMMAND -

The most minute and circumstantial account of this horrible massacre that we recollect to have seen, is given by Mr. Joseph H. Sphon, a native of New Orleans. He was a prisoner with Col. Fannin at Goliad, witnessed his death, and escaped the general massacre in consequence of his being employed as interpreter through the whole of this bloody affair. He was among the passengers in the "Mexican," recently arrived at New Orleans, from Vera Cruz. If his story be true, (and we see nothing in it to induce a suspicion to the contrary) it places the conduct of the Mexicans in a light more revolting, if possible, than previous accounts. We give below an extract in reference to the death of Fannin and the other prisoners. After some particulars respecting the evacuation of Goliad, the attack on Fanin's command by the Mexican cavalry, and their return to Goliad as prisoners of war, — many of which have been already published, Mr. Shpon proceeds as follows: —

"On Palm Sunday, being 27th of March, the prisoners were formed into line, and our informant who was then sleeping in the church (the hospital) being about 6 o'clock in the morning, was called out and told to fall into line; being the last he fell in at the end. They were then marched out of the fort and ranged before the gate, when an officer stepped up and asked Sphon what he was doing there, and ordered him to go back to the hospital where he was wanted, and when on his way was stopped by another officer who told him to order the assistants to have the wounded of the Texians brought in-

to the yard; such as could not walk were to be carried out. Being astonished at these preparations he asked why, when the officer said, "Carts were coming to convey them to Copano, the nearest sea port." The orders of the officers were obeyed, and the wounded brought into the yard, and they were all full of the hope that they were to be shipped to the United States, which had been promised, but their hopes were cruelly blasted when they heard a sudden continued roar of musketry on the outside of the fort, and observed the soldiers wives leap upon the walls and look towards the spot where the report came from. About that time Col. Fannin, who had a room in the church for his use, came out of the church, when a Mexican captain of the battalion called Tres Villas with 6 soldiers came up to Sphon and told him to call Col. Fannin, who firmly walked to the place pointed out by the Mexican captain placing his arm upon the shoulder of Sphon for support, being wounded in the right thigh, from which he was very lame.

All this while, the soldiers were taking the wounded, two at a time, near the gate and setting them down on the ground and bandaging their eyes, would shoot them off, with the same indifference they would a wild animal. There were three soldiers to each two so that after the discharge of two muskets, if death should not have been dealt forth, the third soldier placed the muzzle of the musket near their head or breast and so ended them. When Col. Fannin reached the spot required, the N. W. corner of the fort, Sphon was ordered to interpret the following sentence: — "That for having come with an armed band to commit depredations and revolutionize Texas, the Mexican government was about to chastize him." As soon as the sentence was interpreted to Fannin he asked if he could not see the commandant. The officer said he could not and asked why he wished it. Col. Fannin then pulled forth a valuable gold watch, which he said belonged to his wife, and he wished to present it to the commandant. The captain then said he could not see the commandant, but if he would give him the watch he would thank him — and he repeated in broken English "tank you - me tank you." Col. Fannin told him he might have the watch, if he would have him buried after he was shot, which the captain said should be done — "contod as las formalidadas necessarias" — at the same time smiling and bowing. Col. Fannin then handed him the watch, and pulled out of his right pocket a small bead purse, containing doubloons, the clasp of which was bent; he gave this to the officer, at the same time saying that it had saved his life, as the ball that wounded him has lost part of its force by striking the clasp, which it bent and carried with in into the wounr; a part of a silk hankerchief which he had in his

pocket and which on drawing out drew forth with it the ball. Out of the left pocket of his overcoat, (being cold weather he had on one of India rubber,) a piece of canvas containing a double handful of dollars, which he also gave to the officer. Sphon was then ordered to bandage his eyes, and Col. Fannin handed him the pocket hankerchief. He proceeded to fold it, but being agitated he did it clumsily, when the officer, snatched it from his hand and folded it himself, and told Col. Fannin to sit down on a chair which was near, and stepping behind him bandaged his eyes, says to Col. Fannin in English, "good, good" — meaning if his eyes were properly bound — to which Fannin replied, "yes, yes." The captain then came front and ordered his men to unfix their bayonets and approach Col. Fannin: he hearing them near him, told Sphon to tell them not to place their muskets so near as to scorch his face with the powder. The officer standing behind them after seeing their muskets were brought within two feet of his body, drew forth his hankerchief as a signal, when they fired and poor Fannin fell dead on his right side on the chair, and from thence rolled into a dry ditch about three feet deep, close by the wall."

"The Whole Country Was In Motion"

PHASE #4

THE TEXANS RETREAT . . . ACCOUNT OF THE "RUNAWAY SCRAPE . . . TEXAS NAVY CAPTURES U. S. SHIP BOUND FOR MEXICO WITH SUPPLIES.

THE TROY DAILY WHIG

PRIVATE CORRESPONDANCE FROM TEXAS ...

Extract from a letter, of a late date, from a gentleman in New Orleans to his friend in this city.

"The Texas business is making some noise here at this moment. Santa Anna is driving General Houston before him. The garrisons at La Bahia, or Goliad, as well as that of San Antonio, have been cut off almost to a man. Houston, with a small force, much exaggerated I imagine, is falling back behind the Colorado. My opinion is, they will be nearly exterminated! It has become a war of fanaticism, and they will fight HASTA EL CUCHILLO! There is some danger of our neutrality being compromised in the contest. At all events, our supply of species is cut off, and there is quite a pressure. It may be set down as an undoubted truth, that, with an enormous banking captail here, there is less than a million and a half specie in the city. What do you think of that? If Spain acknowledges the independence of Mexico, Havana and Porto Rico will become the greats of Mexican commerce of the city; indeed, it is felt already.

NEW ORLEANS
COMMERCIAL BULLETIN

LATER FROM TEXAS

By Major Horton, who come passenger in the Texian schooner Invincible, we learn that 1200 Mexicans had crossed the Colorado, 800 men at San Felipe, and 400 at Fort Bend; that General Houston's effective force was 2300. The Colorado has overflowed it's banks, and the 1200 Mexicans cannot retreat. Houston had despatched Maj. Baker with 400 men against 400 Mexicans, and was advancing himself with his whole force upon the Mexican division, whose retreat to the main army was impossible.

The total destruction of the 1200 Mexicans is certain; all was joy and confidence at the seat of the government. The elements are fighting for Texas, and the universal opinion is, that the Mexican army between the Colorado and Brazos is already defeated.

Houston must have fought the battle last Sunday.

LATER STILL

The Texian armed schooner Invincible, Capt. Brown, fell in with the Mexican schooner Montezuma, at anchor off the Brazos Santiago. An action immediately took place, with a running fight for several hours, which terminated in the sinking of the Montezuma before she reached the shore to which she was running. When last seen her yards were under water. She was preparing to convoy to Galveston 1200 men; the expedition is now destroyed.

THE NATIONAL INTELLIGENCER

LATEST FROM TEXAS

The following extracts of a letter from a Virginian who has just returned from the vicinity of Nacodoches, give the latest and most painful accounts of that terror stricken region:

You are aware of my having left home, and seeking the tempestous scenes of Texas, I again put on my sandals, and set forth on my pilgrimage. At Natchitoches I purchased a small black pony; and he preformed admirably. I found no one going the same route. I travelled very rapidly, with nothing to interest or excite me, but conformation of the bloody and perfidious sacrifice of Fannin's men at Goliad. On the 13th. of April, 1836, I road up to a tavern, and whom should I meet but Mr. Wm. S. Archer, Dr. Charles Cook, Mr. Blackburn of Virginia, and Mr. John Morris. They advised me by all means to turn back, and stated that a large band of Indians had united with a Mexican force, and were marching upon Nacogdoches — that the committee of safety had ordered the women and children to retire across the Sabine — and that the men would protect their retreat. I was not quite satisfied at this imminent danger, and after refreshing myself and horse, while the host and his family were zealously packing up for their immediate departure, I road on about ten miles further, and about six from Nacogdoches. — Here I met a bearer of an express, communicating the same intelligence. I made many inquiries, traced the reports to the fountainhead, and was satisfied of their accuracy. The information was derived in this way;

A Mr. Sims, living at the Salines, high up on the river Orphelim, had for a long time traded with the Indians, and was very friendly with them. Bowles, the Cherokee Chief, came to him, and advised him if he had any regard for the lives of his wife and children, to depart instantly, that the Indians and Mexicans were about to "rise-up", and would do tremendous mischief. Sims instantly mounted his horse, and with his family soon left his home behind him. I got all these facts from his own lips. Again, some friendly Indians were sent as spies, and reported the same facts, with a few more details, viz. that the Indians were Comanches and Wittipaus, (Mexican tribes,) piloted by the Caddos. All these were reported at 1,000, and had allied themselves to about 1,700 Mexicans, that the high waters had prevented their marching sooner, but that they would make an immediate decent upon Nacogdoches. I determined to return. The next morning a man without shoes came running into San Augustine, and reported that he had the night before seen 700 Indians in Nacogdoches. He was the very picture of dismay. He had lost his shoes in his alarm and haste. This news flew like wild fire. The whole country was in motion. The main road was strewed with men, women, and children, all joining in one common fight. Everything was given up; their houses left a prey to any passerby, and the most intense stress was exhibeted. I had road twenty miles that morning, without food for my horse or myself. I stopped at a farmer's house, he and his family had just deserted. I entered the house; handsome furniture was scattered over the floor. I found in the kitchen some bread just baking. I made my own breakfast, and feasted my horse on the overflowing corn-crib. — I lit my cigar on the still crackling faggots, and mised on the singular but heart-rending scene just passing before my eyes. I can give you but a feeble idea of the truth. Old men, women and children, all striving which should escape the ruthless savages. Many were on foot, almost broken down by over-exertion and alarm. Many had forgotten the necessary provisions of life, and were now suffering the bitter cravings of appetite. A house had been burnt ACCIDENTLY, and an old Choctaw Indian, perfectly friendly, was seen near it. — This was soon magnified into a horrible picture of the Indians burning houses, the town, and murdering everything before them. You cannot conceive the effect of this news. The river Sabine, at Gaines Ferry, where they had to cross, was very high, and it was necessary to ferry about three- quarters of a mile. This was too far to take them all over, and they had to fall upon the expedient of carring over their women and children, but no MAN, into a little island, where they would be out of harm's way. There was a rumor that the Indians were within two miles of the Sabine, and the scene that followed was one of the most heart-breaking character; The women on the island and on the Texas shore set up a horrid shriek, like the "Damned Spirit's". Never have I witnessed such misery.

"I could not cross at this ferry, but went ten miles down, swam a bad creek and crossed the river. I found a great many people here also. The accounts you can most rely upon are, that the Mexicans and Indians were within twenty miles of Nacogdoches. Their policy, I imagine, is to cut off reinforcements, and hem Houston in. I am fearful about his success. The Mexicans have now some veteran soldiers in the field, and good officers; French, English, and AMERICAN. It is a war of extermination. I am afraid, unless Uncle Sam gives them a helping hand, the Texians will be in a bad situation. By the by, I met Gen. Gaine's troops marching to the Sabine, about 300 in number. He was at the fort examining maps, etc. and does not say whether he will cross the line. He will wait for more men. He has made a requisition for three regiments. I think he will cross the line, and his justification will be, that the Mexicans have been inveigling the AMERICAN Indians to their side, and thus violating the treaty. I hope he may make out a good case! I have never seen the treaty and therefore do not know whether he can be justified."

FURTHER NEWS

The accounts received today from Texas are of a more favorable nature; and negative in part of the previous rumors relative to Nacogdoches. It is true the town had been deserted on the report that the Indians and Mexicans were making a desent upon it; but it was not attacked and not destroyed. Col. Quitman continued there with 200 men; and the Texians having conveyed their families east of the Sabine returned — Some Mexicans had indeed been seen, but they were on their way to join Houston.

Santa Anna was at San Antonio on the 5th. of April. General Houston was at Groce's, west of the Brazos on the 6th., with 2500 men. He was raising horses, or a cavalry of 500 to attack the advance guard of the enemy; encamped within twenty-five miles of him: and had opened communication with the gulf — whence he was supplied with provisions from the Yellowstone and other steamboats. The next arrival may turn the tidings of victory in favor of the Texians.

NEW YORK AMERICAN

LATEST FROM TEXAS

A report was in circulation, at New Orleans, at the beginning of this month, that General Houston had been defeated by the Mexicans.

The New Orleans Bee contradicts it, and says with gravity, that it would be ludicrous, but that it relates to a serious matter, "General Houston has adopted the excellent plan of gradually evacuating the country, and falling back to Nacogdoches and the Sabine, "Till he has Santa Anna's army completely in his power."

The American brig, Jane, Capt. Williams, hence, was seized at Matamoras and the Captain put into prison, for hoisting the American ensign with the union down, as a signal to the American man-of-war which was off that port.

THE NEW ORLEANS BEE

CAPTURE OF THE TEXIAN SCHOONER INVINCIBLE
BY U. S. SLOOP OF WAR -

A CAPTURE: Not long since the Texian armed schooner Invincible, Capt. Brown commander, hailed the American brig Pocket, bound for Matamoras, with provisions and munitions of war for the Mexicans under Santa Anna, as consigned by a house in this city. The Texians finding articles contraband of war in the vessel, altered her course to Galveston; but agreed to pay the Captain even more than the value of the cargo. The Capt. of the Pocket was well satisfied with the arrangements, careless of the destination, provided he and the shippers were paid.

Not so, however, were the shippers. They sent word to Com. Dallas at Pensacola, that a vessel had been siezed on open seas as a prize; and charged the Texians with piracy. Dallas sent out the sloop of war Warren to seize the Invincible; and on Sunday last she was captured off the S.W. pass and brought into port here. When taken the Capt. was not on board; and as many of the crew had mutined, there were only five seamen taken. The others were however subsequently apprehended; and orders given to take them into custody to stand trial for piracy.

"There Is The Enemy . . . Do You Want To Fight?"

PHASE #5

THE BATTLE OF SAN JACINTO . . . SANTA ANNA CAP-
TURED . . . FURTHER REPORTS OF THE BATTLE . . . HOUS-
TON'S REPORT OF THE BATTLE.

NEW ORLEANS BULLETIN

!HIGHLY IMPORTANT FROM TEXAS ! SANTA ANNA CAPTURED AND ! HIS WHOLE FORCE ! HOUSTON VICTORIOUS!

We have been politely favored with the following extract of a letter written to a gentleman in this city, from Natchitoches, which goes still further to corroborate the account received by the Levant, which we publish today.

The substance of which is that an express has arrived here from Natchitoches, from Texan, and is confirmed by General Gaines, that General Houston, of Texas, has conquered Santa Anna and his army. — Santa Anna himself and all his soldiers all prisoners. — The forces of Santa Anna were estimated at 1100; and those of Houston at 600. The express further states that Houston's army destroyed half of the Mexicans, and the loss on his side was 9 killed and 20 wounded.

The saddle of Santa Anna was taken and brought in and is of a costly order, being estimated as worth between 6 and 800 dollars, and the express who brought in the news, rode on the horse of Santa Anna.

All this is indeed cheering news, calculated to arouse all the better feelings, which are implanted in the hearts of those who can rejoice the triumph of freemen over their civil and savage oppressors. — The intelligence received early yesterday morning, and which is also published, will be brought by the Levant, with the scene to be confirmed by the news, difference only that the numbers of the enemy killed and taken by Gen. Houston, vary in amount.

HEADQUARTERS, ARMY,
Army 23, 1836.

TO THE PEOPLE
TOWARDS NACOGDOCHES:

We met Santa Anna on the 21st; we attacked him with 600 men; he had 1100 infantry, two howitzers — we entirely routed his whole force, killed half of his men, and took the rest prisoners. The history of war does not furnish a parallel to the battle. We had 6 killed and 20 wounded. I have not time or I would send on a full report. I will do that in the course of tomorrow. I again call on my fellow citizens to come to the field; let us fall on and conquer the remaining troops, and our country is free; turn out at once, there is no excuse now; let us do the work at once.

THOS. J. RUSK,
Secretary of War.

I certify the above to be a true copy of the express just received from the Secretary of War, who was himself in battle.

A. Houston

The circumstances as related by these gentlemen were that the Mexican army had from some cause or other been separated into two bodits divided by the river Brazos, that the sudden rise of that river prevented the two bodies from effecting a junction — that Houston marched against the larger body amounted to 1300 or 1400 men — that the latter retreated,

!!HIGHLY IMPORTANT FROM TEXAS !! SANTA ANNA CAPTURED AND !! HIS WHOLE FORCE !! HOUSTON VICTORIOUS !!

(CONTINUED)

To J. R. Dunn.

San Augustine,
April 26, 1836

The following is the information which came to hand early yesterday morning —

A gentleman of this city, who arrived this morning from Attakapas states, that on the evening previous to his departure two persons arrived direct from Texas. That these persons, who appeared to be men of respectability, related as a positive fact, that an engagement had taken place between the Texian forces under Gen. Houston, and the Mexican army, in which the latter were totally routed, having lost 700 men in killed and wounded, and 500 prisoners, among whom was Gen. Cos. The loss of the Texians are said to be inconsiderable.

and in their retreat set fire to the town of Harrisburgh. Houston succeeded in overtaking them about 7 miles from that town, and commenced a sudden and vigorous attack on them, and after some severe fighting, the Mexicans were totally defeated, with the loss above mentioned. The gentlemen stated that they were a short distance from Harrisburgh, and could distinctly hear the firing, and that the result was well known before their departure — that Houston had marched in pursuit of the other body which it was supposed could not possibly escape him.

THE NEW ORLEANS BEE

!! GLORIOUS NEWS !!

By the steam-boat Levant which arrived last evening, the accounts are confirmed of Houston's victory over the Mexican army. Having conquered the first division, he attacked the second division under Santa Anna himself — The result of which was hastily communicated in the following circular from the Texican secretary of war to the people of Nacogdoches.

Since writing the above, we heard it stated as if on good authority, that General Houston held a council of war on the fate of his prisoners; **AND THAT SANTA ANNA AND ALL HIS OFFICERS HAD BEEN SHOT!!!** The privates were sent to Matamoros. It was also said that General Gaines had written a private letter confirmatory of this account, but we did not see it. **THERE CAN, HOWEVER, BE NO DOUBT THAT GENERAL HOUSTON HAS CONQUERED; AND THAT THE MEXICANS ARE PROSTRATED!!!** The day of retribution has at length come and Texas is free.

LATE AND IMPORTANT -

Fortune has revolved the spokes of her wheels, and now sides with Texas. Yesterday a gentleman arrived here, and he asserts that two persons had been at St. Martinsville immediately before his departure, who stated as a positive fact, within their own cognizance, that an engagement had taken place between part of the Texican and Mexican army. The latter had been separated into two bodies, divided by the river Brazos, whose sudden rise prevented their junction. The large body consisted of about 1300 to 1400 men, who being attacked by General Houston set fire to the town of Harrisburg and retreated; but Houston succeeded in overtaking them about 7 miles from that place, compelled them to pitched battle, in which 700 of the Mexicans were killed, and 500 taken prisoners — among whom was General Cos, whose "parole d'honneur" will serve him on this occasion! The enemy was completely routed, and the loss of the Texians was very inconsiderable. General Houston immediately marched in pursuit of the other body, and may have equally captured them, but this is not yet ascertained.

NEW ORLEANS BULLETIN

LATEST FROM TEXAS -
CONFIRMATION OF THE CAPTURE OF SANTA ANNA -

The following are copies of letters and documents from Houston's camp, received yesterday by the steamer Levant, from Natchitoches, The orders are copies of translantions from the original Spanish.

SANTA ANNA TO GENERAL FILISOLA, ARMY OF OPERATIONS, COAST DIVISION UNDER MY COMMAND.

Having yesterday had an unfortunate encounter, I have resolved to remain a prisoner of war in the hands of the enemy. After having taken every precaution, I therefore hope that your excellency will cause the division under the command of Gen. Parza to countermarch to Bexar, where he will wait for orders. Your excellency will also return to the same place, and order Gen. Viesca with his division to Gaudalupe Victoria. I have agreed on an armistice with Gen. Houston, ad interim, until we can agree upon terms of lasting peace.

Your excellency will take such measures as may be necessary for the subsistence of the army, which will remain under your command. The money that has arrived at Matamoras, and the provisions of the place, and those at Victoria will be subject to your orders; also 20,000 dollars that may be in the treasury, are to be taken from Bexar. I trust that your excellency will without fail comply with these dispositions, advising me of the same by return of couriers, as also if any should oppose its accomplishments.

God and Liberty.
ANTONIO LOPEZ
DE SANTA ANNA.
Camp Jacinto,
April 22, 1836.

(Copy No. 2.)

Army of Operations.

Excellent Sir — Inasmuch as I have ordered your Excellency by official note of the day that you cause the troops to return to Bexar and Gaudalupe Victoria, I charge you to instruct the commandments of the several divisions, not to permit any damage to be done to the property of the country, hoping that these dispositions will be punctually complied with.

God and Liberty,
ANTONIO LOPEZ
DE SANTA ANNA.
San Jacinto,
April 22, 1836

(Order No. 3.)

Army of Operations.

Excellent Sir, — You will immediately order the military command at Goliad to put all the prisoners made at Copana, at liberty, and send them forthwith to San

Felipe de Austin, and for which purpose your Excellency, will dictate such orders as may be condusive to the object.

God and Liberty,
ANTONIO LOPEZ
DE SANTA ANNA.
Camp San Jacinto,
April 22, 1836.

WAR DEPARTMENT

Headquarters Army,
San Jacinto River,)
April 26, 1836.   )

All the troops on their march from the east, will report at Headquarters as early as possible, marching by way of Harrisburg for the present — but all turn out. The enemy have been badly defeated, and are retreating precipitately for the purpose of contentrating.

One bold push now will drive them entirely out of the country, and secure Liberty, Independence, and Peace of Texas. Let all turn out. Our standard is a victorious one, and waves beautifully under a beneficent providence.

LATER STILL

COPY OF A LETTER FROM
GENERAL HOUSTON

SAN JACINTO,
26 APRIL, 1836

"Tell our friends of the news, and that we have beaten the enemy, Killed 630, and taken 570 prisoners. Generals Santa Anna and Cos are taken, and one General slain; vast amount of property taken, and about 1500 stands of arms, many swords, and one nine pound brass cannon. Tell them to come on, and let the people plant corn."

S. Houston,
Commander-in-Chief

THE NATIONAL INTELLIGENCER

LATE AND IMPORTANT FROM TEXAS -

The following extracts are from official sources:

PORT OF GALVESTON,
April 29, 1836

Colonel Triplet: Dear Sir: You doubtless have heard of the splendid and decisive victory gained on the 21st., April by General Houston over Santa Anna, Col. Almonte, General Cos, and some other officers are prisoners. The enemy had about 600 killed and about 500-600 made prisoners; about thirty officers were killed in the field. Our own loss was 9 killed and 11 wounded. Wonderful disparity!

Our home has been plundered and rifled of everything. We are without any article necessary to housekeeping.

DAVID G. BURNET,
President of the
Republic of Texas

EXTRACT OF ANOTHER LETTER FROM THE CHIEF CLERK OF THE SECRETARY OF THE STATE'S OFFICE, TO E. HALL, ESQ. OF THIS CITY, DATED GALVESTON BAY, APRIL 27, 1836.

I have just had the pleasure of seeing the royal persons, Gen. Santa Anna, General Cos, and Col. Almonte. The battle was fought on the 21st., above Lynch's Ferry; about 650 Mexicans killed, and a like number taken as prisoners. Seven hundred and fifty was the whole of the Texian force. General Houston was slightly wounded.

LOUISIANA ADVERTISER

TEXAS

By the arrival of the schooner Flash, Capt. Howel, from Galveston Bay, yesterday, we learn that Santa Anna was in the charge of Capt. Hawkins, of the the Texian armed schooner Independence, then lying in the bay. Letters from the most respectable sources were also received by this agency, confirming the reported capture of Santa Anna, and furnishing some additional particulars of the battle gained by Gen. Houston. If Santa Anna is really a prisoner, as all accounts go to show, a cessation of hostilities must be consequent on it.

NEW YORK DAILY ADVERTISER

PARTICULARS OF THE TEXIAN VICTORY

Although no official account has been received from General Houston, of his great and astonishing victory, yet no doubt of the fact that he did obtain he said vicory, and that it's results was the capture of the Mexican Chief, can no longer be entertained. But as yet, notwithstanding the number and varity of the accounts that have been received, we are nevertheless in want of the precise fasts and particulars. These are partially supplied by the annexed details, copied from the pages of the Mobile Mercantile Advertiser. They were supplied to that journal by J. Andrews, who has returned from Texas, having been actually engaged in the battle. He has in his possession various documnets from officers high in command, in evidence of the estimation in which he is held on account of his manly deportment during the fight between Col. Ward's command and the Mexicans, as well as in the recent battle between Houston's army and that of Santa Anna. His statement is full of interest, and will not bear abridgement: —

"On the 21st. April, the Texians, under Houston, and 600 strong, had manoeuvred so as to get above and within two miles of the Mexicans, under Santa Anna, who were 1270 strong and near down to the fork of the two rivers — the Brazos and the Sabine. Houston, thus having the enemy snugly hemmed in, had his little army drawn up for the purpose of addressing it in person. "Soldiers," said he, 'there is the enemy — do you want to fight!" "Yes!" was the universal shout. "Well, then," said he, "let us eat our dinner, and then I will lead you into battle!" They obeyed the order to eat, and immediately thereafter at about 4 o'clock, P.M., were marching to the attack. They bore down upon the Mexicans at the top of their speed, reserving their fire until near enough to have every shot tell. A hot engagement was kept up about twenty minuets, when the Mexicans began to break and retreat in great disorder and confusion.

The Texians carried all before them. Although they had but half the numbers of the Mexicans, and but two pieces of cannon of four pounds each, while the enemy had a six and a nine pounder, yet in fifteen minuets after the engagement commenced many of the Mexicans called loudly for quarters. After the route of the Mexicans, Houston's men continued to follow up and pour in upon them for about two hours. — Upwards of 650 Mexicans were killed, and about 600 taken prisoners. There were six or nine Texians killed and about twenty wounded. Generals Cos and Almonte were among the prisoners first taken. The former was pale and greatly agitated, but the latter displayed great coolness and courage, as he had done during the engagement.

Santa Anna fled among the earliest who retreated. He was seen by two boys, one about fifteen and the other about seventeen years of age, to go into a thicket of wood. They kept watch on the place during the night, and the next morning a man came out dressed like a common Mexican soldier. Not suspecting him to be Santa Anna, they took him to General Houston. He was conducted to the officer, where he made himself known as Santa Anna, and asked the respect due officers of rank." Santa Anna, Mr. Andrews says, is about 45 years of age, of rather small stature, dark complexion, black hair, bright eyes, and altogether a good looking man.

When questioned as to the murder of Colonel Fannin and Ward, and the men under their command, he stated that in the battle the evening previous to their surrender, about a 1000 Mexicans were killed, while not more than 20 Texicans had fallen — that the Texicans had exhausted their ammunition, and were without water — that they surrendered upon the terms of capitulation, but that he had been induced to violate those terms for two reasons, first, because the day after the surrender of Col. Ward and those under his command, the number of prisoners became so great in consequence that he had not provisions sufficient for them and his own army; and secondly, that he had not enough men to keep them securely. Consequently, Col. Ward and almost all his soldiers were shot with Col. Fannin.

When questioned respecting the fight near the mission, between the Mexicans and Col. Ward's company, he stated that about 400 Mexicans were killed, but Col. Ward and his men were protected by the walls of the church in which they had stationed themselves.

The following named persons under the command of Colonels Fannin and Ward, made their escape; Lewis Washington, — Dickinson, Horace Bullock, Samuel Hardaway, Benjamin Mordecai,

and Joseph Andrews (our informant), all Georgians. Dr. Shackleford, of Alabama, had his life spared, and is now in attendance upon the wounded Mexicans.

The Mexicans and the Texians who made their escape, agree in stating that when Col. Ward was about to be shot, he was ordered to kneel, but could not be made to do so either by threats or promises. His gallent spirit nothing could subdue. He proudly bid them defiance and died like an American soldier!

In the battle between Houston and Santa Anna, Col. Marabeau B. Lamar, of Georgia, greatly distinguished himself for his valor and intrepidity, and gained the applause of all.

It is said there were not fifty Texians in the battle, that the Texian army was composed almost entirely of volunteers.

Santa Anna is a prisoner on board an armed vessel, near Galveston Island, while the Mexican prisoners, who are able to labor, are engaged in building breastworks on the Island.

The Louisiana Advertiser announces the arrival in New Orleans of the schooner Flash, from Galveston Bay, having on board several passengers who were in the battle of the 21st. of April. She also brought several letters for the Texian agents and for private individuals, all of which fully corroborated the previous accounts of the capture of Santa Anna, and of Houston's unparalleled victory.

When the Flash sailed Santa Anna was under the charge of Capt. Hawkins, of the Texian schooner of war Independence, then in Galveston Bay, and the prisoners of

91

his army were employed in building Fort Travis, on Galveston Island. (This New Orleans item corroborates the preceeding statement of Mr. Andrews, at Mobile.)

The accounts of the Flash state, that General Houston had great difficulty in restraining his troops from proceeding summarily with Santa Anna, as the Texians made their attack under the watchwords of "REMEMBER THE ALAMO AND FANNIN."

Asked why he put the survivors of the Alamo to death, Santa Anna replied that his troops were so much exasperated at the number of their killed and wounded, that he could not restrain them. He was then asked why Fannin's command was slaughtered. His answer was, there were so many prisoners that it was impossible to either keep them or feed them. — He also asserted that Col. Fannin and Dr. Shackelford still remained prisoners at Victoria.

THE NEW ORLEANS BEE

TEXAS

The glorious news we have is official, and can be relied on. Had Santa Anna concentrated his two divisions, Houston would have lost the day. — The latter General has to encounter now the two divisions under Sesma!

- POSTSCRIPT -

12 o'clock, 3rd. May, 1836, — Mail closing. — Dear Sir — The steamboat Romee has just arrived from Quichita, Red River, and confirms the report brought by the steamer Lavant, and we have just seen a letter from General Houston, dated 20th, April, 1836, a few hours previous to the battle. He states that Santa Anna is in the field and that he (Houston) had one half of his men in ambush in order to coax Santa Anna on and give him battle. There can be no doubt that Santa Anna is taken, as reported. No one doubts it here.

NEW YORK COMMERCIAL BULLETIN

BATTLE OF SAN JACINTO

At last General Houston's official statement is forthcoming. We find it in the New Orleans Bee, to which it was probably communicated by the General, and for which we presume that it was written, although it was written and dated at San Jacinto, and addressed to the President of Texas. It gives very little information that is new, but must be copied, we suppose, as part of the authentic history of war.

HEADQUARTERS OF THE ARMY, SAN JACINTO,

25 April, 1836.

TO HIS EXCELLENCY
D. G. BURNETT,
PRESIDENT OF
THE REPUBLIC OF TEXAS —

Sir — I regret extreamly that my situation since the battle of the 21st has been such as to prevent my rendering you any official report of the same, previous to that time.

I have the honor to inform you, that on the evening of the 18th inst. after a forced march of fifty-five miles, which was effected in two days and a half, the army arrived opposite Harrisburgh; that evening a courier of the enemy was taken, from whom I learned that General Santa Anna, with one division of his choice troops had marched in the direction of Lynche's Ferry on the San Jacinto, burning Harrisburgh as he passed down. The army was ordered to be in readiness to march early on the next morning. The main body effected a crossing over Buffalo Bayou, below Harrisburgh, on the morning of the 19th, having left the sick, and a sufficient camp guard in the rear.

We continued our march through the night, making but one half mile in the prairie, and without refreshment. At daylight we resumed the line of march, and in a short distance our scouts encountered those of the enemy, and we received information that Gen. Santa Anna was at New Washington, and would that day take up the line of march for Anahuac, crossing at Lynche's. The Texan army halted within half a mile of the ferry in some timber, and we were engaged in slaughtering beeves, when the army of Santa Anna was discovered to be approaching in battle array, having been encamped at Clopper's Point, eight miles below. — Disposition was immediately made of our forces, and preparation for his reception. He took a position with his infantry, and artillery in the center, occupying an island of timber, his cavalry covering the left flank. The artillery, consisting of one double fortified medium brass twelve pounder then opened on our encampment. The infantry in column advanced with the design of charging our lines, but were repulsed by a discharge of grape and cannister, from our artillery, consisting of two six pounders. The enemy had occupied a piece of timber within rifle shot of the left wing of our army, from which an occasional interchange of small arms took place between the troops, until the enemy withdrew to a position on the bank of the San Jacinto, about three quarters of a mile from our encampment, and commenced fortification.

A short time before sunset, our mounted men about eighty-five in number under the special command or Col. Sherman, marched out for the purpose of reconnoitering the enemy. While advancing, they received a volley from the left of the enemy's infantry, and after a sharp encounter, with their cavalry, in which ours acted extreamly well, and performed some feats of daring chivalry, they retired in good order having had two men severely wounded, and several horses killed. In the meantime the infantry under the command of Lieut. Col. Millard, marched out for the purpose of covering the retreat of the cavalry if necessary. All then fell back in good order to our encampment about sunset, and remained there without any istensible action until the 21st., at half past three o'clock, taking the first refreshment which they had enjoyed in two days. The enemy in the meantime extended the right flank of their infantry so as to occupy the extreme point of a skirt of timber on the bank of the San Jacinto, and secured their left by a fortification about five feet high, constructed of packs and baggage, leaving an opening in the center of the breatwork in which their artillery was placed, their cavalry upon their left wing.

About 9 o'clock on the morning of the 21st, the enemy were reinforced by 500 choice troops, under the command of General Cos, increasing their effective force to upwards of 1500 men, while our aggregate force for the field numbered 783. At half-past three o'clock in the evening. I ordered the officers of the Texian army to parade their respective commands, having in the meantime ordered the bridge on the only road communicating with the Brazos, distance eight miles from our encampment, to be destroyed, thus cutting off all possibility of escape. — Our troops paraded with alarcity and spirit, and were anxious for the contest. Their conscious disparity in numbers seemed only to increase their anxiety for the conflict. Our situation afforded me an opportunity of making the arrangements preparatory to the attack, without exposing our designs to the enemy. The 1st. Regiment, commanded by Col. Burleson, was assigned the center. The 2nd. Regiment, under the command of Col. Sherman, formed the left wing of the army. The Artillery, under the special command of Col. Geo. W. Hockley, Inspector General, was placed on the right of the 1st. Regiment; and four companies of infantry, under the artillery upon the right. Our Cavalry, sixty-one in number, commanded by Col. M. B. Lamar, (whose gallent and daring conduct on the previous day had attracted the admiration of his comrades, and called him to that station), placed on our extreme right, completed our line. Our cavalry was first despatched to the front of the enemy's left, for the purpose of attracting their notice, while an extensive island of timber afforded us an opportunity of concentrating our forces and displaying from that point, agreeably to the previous design of the troops. Every evolution was performed with alarcity, the whole advancing rapidly in line, and through an open prairie, with-

BATTLE OF SAN JACINTO
(CONTINUED)

out any protection whatever for our men. The artillery advanced, and took station within two hundred yards of the enemy's breastwork, and commenced an effective fire with grape and cannister.

Col. Sherman with his regiment, having commenced the action upon our left wing, the whole line, at the center and on the right, advancing in double quick time, rung the war cry, "REMEMBER THE ALAMO," received the enemy's fore and advancing within point blank range before a piece was discharged from our lines. Our line advanced without a halt, until they were in possession of the woodland and the enemy's breastwork. The right wing of Burleson's and the left of Millard's, taking possession of the breastwork; our artillery having gallently charged up within 70 yards of the enemy's cannon, when it was taken by our troops. The conflict lasted about eighteen minuets from the time of close action, until we were in possession of the enemy's encampment, taking one piece of cannon, (loaded,) four stands of colors, all their camp equipage, stores and baggage. Our cavalry had charged and routed that of the enemy upon the right, and given pursuit to the fugitives, which did not cease until they arrived at the bridge which I have mentioned before, Capt. Karnes, always the foremost in danger, commanding the pursuers. The conflict at the breastwork lasted but a few moments; many of the troops encountered hand to hand, and not having the advantage of bayonets on our side, our riflemen used their pieces as war clubs, breaking many of them off at the breech. The route commenced at half-past 4, and the pursuit by the main army continued until twilight.

A guard was then left in charge of the enemy's encampment, and our army returned with their killed and wounded. In the battle, our loss was two killed and twenty-three wounded, six of whom mortally. The enemy's loss was 630 killed, among which was 1 General, 4 Colonels, 2 Lieut. Cols., 5 Capts., 12 Lieuts. Wounded 208. Prisoners 730 — President Santa Anna, General Cos, 4 Cols., aids to General Santa Anna, 6 Lieut. Cols., the private secretary to Santa Anna, and the Colonel of the Guerrero Battalion, are included in the number. General Santa Anna was not taken until the 22nd, and Gen. Cos on yesterday, very few having escaped. About 600 muskets, 300 sabers, and 200 pistols, have been collected since the action; several hundred mules and horses were taken, and near twelve thousand dollars in specie. For several days previous to the action, our troops were engaged in forced marches, exposed to excessive rains, and the additional inconvenience of extremely bad roads, illy supplied with rations and clothing — yet amid every difficulty they bore up with cheerfulness and fortitude, and preformed their marches with spirit and alacrity — there was no murmuring.

Previous to and during the action, my staff evinced every dispostion to be useful, and were actively engaged in their duties. In the conflict I am assured that they demeaned themselves in such a manner as proved them worthy members of the army of San Jacinto. Col. T. J. Rusk, Sec. of War, was on the field. For weeks his services had been highly beneficial to the army; in the battle he was

BATTLE OF SAN JACINTO
(CONTINUED)

on the left wing, where Col. Sherman's command first encountered and drove the enemy; he bore himself gallently, and continued his efforts and activity, remaining with the pursuers until resistance ceased.

For the Commanding General to attempt discrimination as to the conduct of those who commanded in the action, or those who were commanded, would be impossible. Our success in the action is conclusive proof of their daring intrepidity and courage; every officer and man proved himself worthy of the cause in which he battled, while the triumph received a lustre from the humanity which characterised their conduct after victory, and richly entitles them to the admiration and gratitude of their General. Nor should we withhold the tribute of our grateful thanks from that Being who rules the destinies of nations, and has in the time of greatest need enabled us to arrest a powerful invader while devastating our country.

I have the honor to be,
With high consideration,
Your obedient servant,

SAM HOUSTON,
Commander-in-Chief

"March! To Avenge God! Your Country! And Your President!"

PHASE #6

MEXICANS ON THE RETREAT FROM TEXAS . . . FILISOLA AGREES TO LEAVE TEXAS . . . A TREATY WITH SANTA ANNA . . . HOUSTON MAY DIE OF WOUND RECEIVED IN BATTLE . . . TEXAS STILL ASKS FOR VOLUNTEERS . . . SANTA ANNA UNDER STRONG GUARD AT VELESCO . . . MEXICAN TROOPS AT SAN ANTONIO . . . GENERAL HOUSTON RECOVERED . . . SANTA ANNA'S VINDICATION . . . MEXICAN TROOPS LEAVE SAN ANTONIO . . . ACCOUNT OF THE MEXICAN RETREAT . . . MEXICO PREPARING TO INVADE TEXAS . . . PROCLAMATION OF JOSE CORRO . . . FILISOLA CENSURED BY MEXICAN CONGRESS.

THE NEW ORLEANS BEE

FROM TEXAS

The rumor via Natchitoches, that twelve hundred Mexicans, one division of the army under Colonel Woll, had surrendered themselves prisoners of war to between three and four hundred Texans, agreeably to the request of Santa Anna, that they should lay down their arms is confirmed.

It was also stated that the Texican force under Col. Burleson has overtaken the main division of the Mexican Army under Filisola and Sesma, when crossing the Colorado, and that the Mexicans merely requested to be undisturbed in their retreat from Texas. And further, that they had thrown into the river a large quantity of ammunition, lest it should fall into the hands of the Texans. It is added that the latter have pursued the prudential policy of building a bridge for the escape of the enemy, who are nearly three to one.

It is further stated that a large number of Texans had visted the Mexican camp on the Colorado, and slept there one night, and had been treated more as men whom they looked upon as already their conquerors than captives, which they had it in their power to make them had they been so inclined. Our informant says he has been assured by those persons after their return to the Texan camp from this visit, that the Mexicans said openly, if the Texans would only allow them to return unmolested, that they would never trouble them again.

TROY DAILY WHIG

TEXAS -

A gentleman of high respectability, who arrived in this city last evening, informs us that Joseph Baker, formerly the editor of the Telegraph, printed at San Felipe, having been sent, after the battle of San Jacinto, to the Mexican army, left the division under the command of Filisola, at the Colorado.

Filisola observed to Mr. Baker, that as General Santa Anna was a prisoner, he did not acknowledge him as general of the forces then in the field, but would recognize him as President of the Mexican nation, and as such he would obey his order to withdraw the troops, and would exercise it as soon as possible.

He said that he had no doubt but Congress would acknowledge the independence of Texas, for it is a country the Mexican people did not want; and although it had been explored and known to them for 150 years, and although a good country for the agriculturist, it was not one adopted to the habits of the Mexican people, there being too many flies and mosquitoes for the convenience of raising stock.

He asknowledged the the present campaign in Texas had terminated to the great disgrace of Mexico — that the cruel massacre of Col. Fannin's division was unjustifiable, and would meet with the just indignation of the civilized world. He further said, that the invasion of Texas was alone projected and carried on by the ambition of Santa Anna; that had it not been for this, Texas would have been admitted a state of the Mexican Republic at the time she made the application through her agent, Gen. S. F. Austin, in 1833, and at this time would have had a local government suited to her wants.

THE NEW ORLEANS BEE

LATE FROM TEXAS

News arrived in town yesterday from Galveston, stating that the Texican Government had effected a negotiation or treaty with Santa Anna, as the President General of Mexico.

We have not ascertained the particulars of this treaty; but it is supposed that it will recognize Texas as an independent nation. Whether this will be done by Mexico, or whether it should be tolerated by the United States, is doubtful. The Texican war is national in Mexico; and was more involuntary than voluntary with Santa Anna. The latter was obliged to continue his own popularity and power: so that whether he be liberated, held captive or shot, the war will be continued, and may not be concluded for months or years!

THE BALTIMORE GAZETTE

!! GENERAL HOUSTON MAY DIE !!

"General Houston is in very bad health, and without good attention I fear will lose his life — his wound in the foot is very bad, and think must mortify. He is quite unable to stand, and fainted yesterday, when a little fatigued." We trust that the above may not be true, or that it is at least exaggerated. — The above information was received via letter from New Orleans dated June 2d. 1836.

THE NEW ORLEANS BEE

MORE MEN NEEDED IN TEXAS!!

An address from General Rusk, in command at present of the Texian forces, called vigorously upon friends in the U. S. for aid. "You may be told," he says, "as you have been before told, that the war is at an end, that there is not further need of men, — IT IS NOT SO! The people of Texas, a small number of men, struggling for the sacred principals of human liberty, need your assistance. We present to you a field where daring and enterprising bravery may measure arms with a hireling soldiery, who are warring against the sacred rights of men, and have dyed their unhallowed hands in the best blood of the United States. — Come then to our assistance, and let us plant our standard in the defiance of the yoke of tyranny, upon the Rio Grande."

The forces of the Mexicans still in Texas, is estimated in this address at 5000. The Texian army, though "little over one tenth of the number," were advancing upon them.

NEW ORLEANS
COMMERCIAL BULLETIN

LATE FROM TEXAS

The Texian armed schooner Independence, commanded by Charles E. Hawkins, seven days from Velasco Texas, anchored yesterday below the point, and fired a salute of 14 guns. P. W. Grayson, and James Collingsworth, Esqs. came in here as passengers. These gentlemen are clothed with full powers to negociate with our government for the recognition of the independence of Texas, and will leave tomorrow for the city of Washington with that view.

From these gentlemen, we learn that an armistice has been entered into between the Texian and the Mexican commander in chief Filisola, and that the remains of the Mexican army are by this time on the opposite side of the Rio Grande, rejoiced doubtless at their escape from the Texians, and firmly resolved never again to face a Texian rifle. Santa Anna remains strongly guarded at Velasco, from whence he has no chance of escape and will be retained there with the other prisoners, until communications shall be received from the Mexican Government. Until then, the fate of the Texian invader will be kept secret. If Congress has not ere this recognized the independence of Texas, we entertain little doubt as to its consumation, upon the arrival at Washington of the Commissioners. Would that upon the joyful commemoration of our Fourth of July, we could at the same time rejoice in the effectual recognition of the independence of our sister republic of Texas.

THE NEW ORLEANS BEE

TEXAS

We confirm the previous reports that the Mexican troops had concentrated at San Antonio. About one thousand volunteers from the United States, had arrived in Texas. Generals Santa Anna and Almonte were still at Velasco; the other prisoners at Galveston Island. The Texans are said to be very urgent in demanding, or at least desiring to have Santa shot immediately.

MOBILE CHRONICAL

IMPORTANT FROM TEXAS -

We learn the important fact of the departure of General Houston for the Texian army, his wound having almost entirely recovered. This will be as unexpected and as fearful intelligence to some as it is heart cheering to others, and as we believe fortunate and happy for Texas. General Houston politely declined the kind invitation of his friends in New Orleans to a public dinner on the honorable objection that he ought not appear on any festive occasion, while there was an enemy remaining in his adopted country.

The Mexican Government, not discouraged by the defeat of their troops, were preparing to send a large army into Texas, in which event Santa Anna and the prisoners would be put to death. A letter from Galveston Island Roads, says that Cos is much hurt by the bitterness of the language used in the American newspapers against Santa Anna and himself. He also felt remorse of his conscious keenly stung by various persons visiting him that he had killed a father, a son, or a brother. He is under well grounded apprehensions that he will soon be shot, which would be, however, a poor punishment for his crimes. The Texian army had crossed the Colorado, and were on their march Westward.

NEW ORLEANS BULLETIN
SANTA ANNA'S VINDICATION

The following is a translation of a document presented by Gen. Santa Anna to the Executive government of Texas, with a request that it be published. The request has been complied with by the government. In answer to the same, and that the public may appreciate the motives of Santa Anna, we give the additional communication, with the single observation, that did the paper require it, many affidavits could be produced to prove a written capitulation. The part of the document of Santa Anna, will strike our readers, as differing somewhat from the true character of his subjects.

PRIVATE SECRETARY OF THE PRESIDENT OF THE REPUBLIC OF MEXICO, GENERAL IN CHIEF OF THE ARMY OF OPERATIONS.

In the journal entitled "El Correo Atlantico," of New Orleans, which has fallen into my hands; which, although dictated by vengence, as may be perceived at first sight, I cannot refrain from noticing the injury done to the Mexican army, by attributing to it actions of which it is incapable.

It is said in an article relating to the event respecting Col. Fannin, that which follows —

This chief, according to the orders received from General Houston, left Goliad on the 19th. of March, with 350 volunteers, and at a distance of eight miles east from that spot, found himself surrounded by 2000 of Santa Anna's infantry and cavalry, who, after having destroyed his little advance guard, which consisted of 58 men, attacked him between 4 and 5 in the afternoon, and were repulsed with the loss of 10 killed and wounded, the loss of the Texians being insignificant; night coming on Fannin marched to a more suitable position, where he entrenched.

The Santa Annists despairing of conquering him by an attack face to face, had recourse, as usual, to deception, and on the following morning they hoisted a flag of truce. Fannin then went to converse, halfway between his camp and that of the traitors, with their chief, who stated to him that he was aquainted with the smallness of his forces; that they were in a plain destitute of water, and surrounded; but he was willing to grant them quarter, etc. Fannin fell into the snare and capitulated. According to the agreement his troops were to lay down their arms, return to Goliad and remain there some days until they could embark at Copano for New Orleans. All this was done, but on the ninth day after their arrival at Goliad, they were informed that a vessel was ready at Copano to receive them; they were then accordingly marched out between two files of VALIENTES, who, at a distance of five miles from Goliad, fired upon them and assassinated them all, excepting Mr. Hudden and three others, who fled precipitatley to a bush, where they remained until able to put themselves in safety, etc.

To these assertions I can observe that the Mexican troops who defeated Fannin, did not raise a flag of truce, nor did their chief give any assurance of quarter by celebrating a capitulation in consequence of such an offer. To affirm facts of so much importance, it is necessary to have an evidence of them, and I am certain that they could never be proved.

The report I received from General Don Jose Urrea, who commanded in that action, was to the effect: that finding himself in front of Goliad, (where Fannin was with his party) he was told that the enemy had undertaken a retreat towards Victoria, a circumstance he had not before preceived, on account of the thick fog; and that he proceeded to join them, which he subsequently effected on the plain called "Encinul del Pedido," and fought until dark; that on the following day a part of his artillery and infantry arrived, with which he continued to attack; — which having been observed by Fannin, and considering his loss as certain, hoisted a flag of truce, and sent a paper written with a pencil, containing some articles offering to surrender if his life should be warrented, etc. to which General Urrea returned a negative answer, adding, that if they did not surrender immediately, he would continue firing upon them. Fannin then surrendered, by throwing down his arms, and they all remained in the power of General Urrea, who sent the prisoners and wounded to Goliad, and he continued his route to Victoria.

This is the substance of General Urrea's report, as can be seen in the "Diario del Gobiernoi" of Mexico, the ORIGINAL having been sent by me to the Minister of War, as it was my duty to inform his Excellency the President AD INTERIM of the Republic.

The commandant of Goliad, made me acquainted with the con-flagration of the town, executed by Fannin on his starting from the fort, not one house having been left for the shelter of the inhabitants; and with the indignation of the latter at the loss of their cattle, together with other vexations, they were reduced to a most sad situation; and communicated to me subsequently his having applied the circular of the Supreme Government to those who were comprehended in it, with the exception of 86 individuals who had come from New Orleans, taken in Copano on account of their having surrendered their arms at the first summons.

Although we knew that the object of that party was to join Fannin, for which motive they came armed, I ordered them to be kept as prisoners, as was effectively done. I gave the same order respecting other individuals taken in the remaining divisions, and they will manifest the treatment they have experienced.

THE MEXICANS, IN EVERY EPOCH, HAVE GIVEN REPEATED PROOF OF THEIR GENEROSITY, AS THEY ARE NATURALLY HUMANE AND COMPASSIONATE! If some military chiefs have fulfilled the express orders of their government, to whom they owe obedience, they do not merit for this any DIATRIBE or charge whatever. — When governments determine about some matter, they must have their reasons, and to them alone it belongs to be answerable to the world for their actions; and in this persuasion, I omit to examine if the circular I have quoted as dictated by the government of the Mexican Republic, applied to

SANTA ANNA'S VINDICATION

(CONTINUED)

Fannin and his men, was founded or not upon justice.

This being the true exposition of what has taken place in this matter, which has induced me to take the pen, I will be obliged to your Excellency to order this manifestation to be published, to avoid equivocations which might stain the good name of the army to which I belong, protesting to your Excellency, on the occasion, the considerations of my esteem.

God and Liberty!
Velasco, May 23, 1836

ANTONIO LOPEZ
DE SANTA ANNA

PHILADELPHIA GAZETTE

TEXAS

The following is an account of the retreat of the Mexican army from Texas . . .

Natchitoches,
June 13, 1836

"By three gentleman of Virginia, who reached here from our army yesterday, we have news up to the first of this month, when our army was near La Bahia. The enemy had passed there, which was the last place there was any apprehension of their making a stand. The Mexican division at San Antonio had been insulted by the Comanches in that place who took from them all their horses and mules and left them with no means to retreat. The enemy spiked all the cannon and threw them in the river, blew up the Alamo, left San Antonio, and joined the main army at La Bahia, as they have no means of conveying their baggage, to enable them to leave be a more direct route for Mexico. The main army on their retreat between the Colorado and San Bernard, lost in one bog upwards of 100 mules, 14 baggage waggons, and made causeways of their muskets to get over the morasses, — burnt the carriages of their cannon, and also buried their guns. This is a true account of the glorious retreat of the Mexican army, consisting of between 4000 and 5000 men, who fled thus, least they might be overtaken by our army of 6 or 700 men. The enemy have now left our country, San Antonio is entirely deserted by it's citizens. They say there are not six souls in this place."

THE TROY DAILY WHIG

TEXAS

Extract from a letter from Col. Sterling C. Robertson, of Texas, to his friend in Nashville; dated May 26, 1836, at San Augustine, Texas.

I am sent on here, by the commanding general, to try and raise some recruits for the army which is now on its march to San Antonio; at which place there are some fears, that the Mexican army, may make another stand; though they have been ordered by Santa Anna to march out of the country, to Monte Del Ray, in the State of Nueva Leon. The panic prevalent among the citizens of Texas, was not to be compared with that of the Mexican army, when they heard of the defeat, and capture of Santa Anna, Cos, Almonte, &c. I went in pursuit of those that escaped from the field of battle, and those that were in the rear of the reinforcement, commanded by Cos; and left as a guard for his baggage. They appeared to have been frightened almost to death. Every hundred yards on the road, for 20 miles they had thrown away some of their plunder, and a whole mule load could have been collected, frequently in the distance of a mile; and often the mule with his pack on his back, being run down, was left on the road side. They left the main road, and went through the prairie; and travelled all night, to enable them to reach the Brazos; where the division of Sesma lay, or was crossing the river, at a place called Fort Bend; about 40 miles below San Felipe.

I there joined a detachment of mounted men, and went on a reconnoitering trip, in pursuit of Sesma and Filisola, on their retreat out of the country. From every appearance presented, by the scattered baggage, muskets thrown away, and mules left bogged in the mud, the panic appeared even greater than among the fugitives from the field of battle. They left 50 mules and 14 baggage wagons in the mud in the distance of ten miles; buried one piece of cannon, and threw at least 1000 stand of arms in the river San Bernard. When the advance of the detachment came up with them, they said they were getting out of the country as fast as they could, and would obey the orders of Santa Anna, and go to Monte Del Rey, by way of San Antonio. We could have taken at least 1000 men of them, with their mules and baggage and cannon, if we had been allowed to do so, but as the treaty was on hand, we were ordered not to molest them.

If I had the command, I would have endeavored to have misconstrued my orders, and at least taken their cannon, and arms from them. They had ten pieces of cannon, six pounders: and an immense quantity of plunder, which they had taken from the houses of the citizens of Texas, after they had left them. Our men were all anxious for the contest; flushed with victory, and full of resentment against the Mexicans. On the other side, the officers and soldiers, were nearly frightened to death; and would have surrendered, in one moment, and I think without the firing of a gun. I have no doubt Gen. Rusk regrets that it was not done, as nothing has been done with regard to the treaty; and he is now on his march after them to

107

San Antonio; at which place I expect, we shall have them to fight, unless we can show a respectable army. If we do I think they will acknowledge our independence. Two expresses in the last two days, have gone on from Gen. Gaines, to the headquarters of the Texan and Mexican armies. Some thinks he offers the mediation of the United States between the parties, and others that the United States have bought the country. —

Yours respectfully —

STERLING C. ROBINSON.

THE PENSACOLA GAZETTE
IMPORTANT FROM MEXICO

The U. S. cutter Jefferson, under the command of Capt. Jackson, arrived here, twelve days from Tampico. All intercourse was forbidden there between vessels of war and the shore. Merchant vessels are permitted to enter the harbor but not to leave. This seems to be the case at present, at all Mexican ports. While the Jefferson lay off shore, intelligence was received at Tampico of the capture of Santa Anna — The flags of the vessels in port and of the fortifications were hoisted at half-mast, in sign of mourning for the event.

Active preparations were making to assemble a large military force to march upon Texas. Every department of Mexico was required to furnish its quota of troops for this service, to be assembled at Matamoras. Much excitement prevailed among the inhabitants of all classes. Apprehensions were entertained that Santa Anna and his fellow prisoners had been put to death by the Texians, and resolutions were publicly adopted and promulgated by the provisional government, that no act or concession of Santa Anna to the Texians, while a prisoner, should be regarded as valid. Capt. Jackson was not even permitted to communicate with Mr. Robertson, our Consul at Tampico, except through the Commanding General Gomez.

NEW ORLEANS BULLETIN

LATE FROM MEXICO

By the arrival of the schooner Caleb Goodwin from Vera Cruz, we have received information from Mexico, which states that the clerical and military portion were panic struck at hearing of the defeat of the presumed invincible Santa Anna and his battalions, which came like a thunder-bolt. The government papers charge General Gaines with aiding the "rebel troops."

There is a strong probability of a revolution in Mexico and the re-establishment of the constitution of 1824. The restoration of Santa Anna, should he be permitted to return, is quite out of the question.

By a letter from Mexico we learn that the Americans there are daily abused in the public prints and threats made of taking their property, and of making them pay for the expenses of the Texian War.

It is untrue that there are two pirate vessels fitting out at Jamaica to aid the Mexicans.

THE TROY DAILY WHIG

MEXICO AND TEXAS

By the arrival at New York of the Steam Packet from Charleston, later intelligence from Mexico and Texas has been received. The articles between Santa Anna and the Texian Government have been made public. An American officer on board the U.S. Schooner Grampus has written a letter containing the following information:

By an act of congress received at Tampico on the 18th. of May, 1836, it was decreed —

1st. That the government would not accede to any act or treaty made by Santa Anna, during his imprisonment in Texas.

2d. That every state in the republic should furnish forthwith, one forth of her forces to be equipped and ordered to march as soon as possible to Matamoras.

3d. That all flags throughout the republic should be worn at half mast, during the imprisonment of the President.

On the first of June, 1836, intelligence was received that all parts of the republic were closed against the sailing of all merchant vessels, and against communication of whatsoever nature, with all vessels of war. This last act of the Mexican government, as it is well understood, has been particularly directed against the United States, with whom there appears to be the most bitter animosity. Most of the foreign inhabitants of Tampico were in daily fear of losing their lives, as it is publicly declared that all foreign houses will be robbed, and the inhabitants butchered, as soon as it should be ascertained that Santa Anna had been shot.

Warlike preparations are making in every direction, and it is current among the officers of the army, that 17,000 men were to march against Texas. Some of which are on their march for their headquarters — Matamoras. It is probable that they cannot raise that number by 4 or 5000, nor are they, when called troops, are they disciplined, but farmers, mule-drivers, etc. taken by force wherever they can be found — however, a desperate struggle will be made by Mexico to regain Texas. Let them, therefore, be on guard, as the strictest precautions are taken to prevent them from having any knowledge of their military movements. Jose Marie Corro is President, and promises to sell the crucifixes from the churches to carry on the war, if means cannot otherwise be had.

Intelligence has been received at New Orleans from the city of Mexico, by way of Matamoras, that General Urrea had been appointed Generalisimo of the Mexican army against Texas, and it was reported that the congress and government had resolved to ABANDON SANTA ANNA TO HIS FATE! This latter rumor is discredited. It was also reported that Urrea had been authorized to raise an army of 15,000 men; and that $600,000 had been raised in one day by subscription in the city of Mexico to furnish them with equipments.

From Texas we learn that the Indians had attacked the Texian settlements at the head waters of the Brazos, and committed several murders. Gen. Green and Felix Houston had marched against them with 600 men — the effective force of Texas now in the field is about 2000 men. General Rusk was at Goliad with 600 men; his advance post extended to the Rio Del Norte, and had quite possession of the sea-voast.

General Filisola had received positive orders from the Mexican government to cease retreating, to recruit his forces, and again oppose the Texians in conjunction with Urrea. The latter has established his headquarters at Matamoras, and has with him 3,000 men. — Filisola will be stationed in the west.

Two Texian officers had arrived at Matamoras, to negociate for an exchange of prisoners.

PROCLAMATION . . .

The President of the Republic (pro tempore) to the warriors of the Mexican army . . .

SOLDIERS — One of the events very frequent in war has placed in the power of the enemy to our independence, the heroic conqueror of Tampico, the President of the Republic, your General-in-Chief, the idol of our hearts, the immortal, Santa Anna! Excited by the ardor of glory, and a vehement desire to terminate the campaign, by one blow, his excellency escorted a petty force of the army which remains untouched; and this force having been beaten by superior numbers, this illustrious genius, whose exploits form the most brilliant page in our history, has lost his own liberty in endeavouring to secure that of his country.

Our mourning has commenced; the fatal day of the 21st. of April, 1836, and since then, displays the vengenance that should prevail in all Mexican hearts. SOLDIERS, our grief is immense; but it will not be useless. For the liberty of the President and for the honor of the nation, the government will raise all possible resources; they will be boundless; and my desire is to employ them without restriction, without delay, without hesitation; for I know my duty and will fulfill it. Misfortune to the enemy of our country! The foreign will be vanquished, and the domestic exemplary punished, if any such shall dare assist in this sacred war of the country, the criminal desires of the Texian rebels.

FRIENDS! A momentary adversity should not discourage the constant protection of our rights. To you, soldiers, — you have proved the vicissitudes of fortune, to leave to the world the remembrance of virtue, honor, and courage; and in invoking the providence who rules the destiny of nations.

MARCH! TO AVENGE GOD! YOUR COUNTRY! AND YOUR PRESIDENT!

JOSE JUSTO CORRO
Mexico, 19th. May, 1836

THE TROY DAILY WHIG
MEXICO

It appears by the late news from Mexico that the conduct of General Filisola, the officer in command of the army after the capture of Santa Anna, has been severely censured by the Mexican Congress and the people for obeying the orders of the captive General. The Texian war is popular in Mexico, and under the present aspect of affairs, the Texains will have to encounter the whole power of the Mexican Government in their efforts to maintain their independence.

"...The People Are Quietly Cultivating Their Land."

PHASE #7

BURNET URGES ALL MEN TO ENLIST IN ARMY . . . FILISOLA
ORDERED TO MEXICO . . . TEXAS ARMY BURIES REMAINS
OF FANNIN'S COMMAND . . . LAMAR ADDRESSES TEXAS
SOLDIERS . . . ATTEMPT MADE TO SHOOT SANTA ANNA . . .
MEXICAN ARMY DESERTING RANKS . . . FILISOLA SUR-
RENDERS HIMSELF FOR TRIAL . . . SANTA ANNA HELD AT
COLUMBIA . . . NO FURTHER TROUBLE FROM MEXICANS
EXPECTED . . . CHARGE OF TREASON AGAINST BURNET . . .
ATTEMPT TO FREE SANTA ANNA . . . HOUSTON ELECTED
PRESIDENT . . . MEXICAN TROOPS STILL DESERTING . . .
A VIEW OF THE REVOLUTION.

THE NEW ORLEANS COURIER

TEXAS

President Burnet of Texas exhorts the people of Texas to be united in their movements against the enemy. Every able bodied man in Texas over 16 and under 50, is to enroll immediately for duty. — Each company of 56 men is to elect their officers, and to march forthwith to headquarters.

A list of all able to bear arms, whether absent or present, to be reported by each muncipality of the War Department.

All officers or men on furlough to return immediately to duty, on pain of forfeiting their commissions and bounties.

NEW YORK COURIER AND INQUIRER
MEXICO

We received at a late hour last night a file of Vera Cruz papers to the 1st July, and the Diario del Gobierno, of the city of Mexico. The latter paper contains the only article of importance. They consist of an official despatch from the Mexican General, Vicento Filisola, detailing the proceedings of the Mexican army in Texas, until the capture of Santa Anna, the subsequent proceedings under the convention for the evacuation of Texas concluded between Santa Anna and President Burnet, the adhesion given by Filisola to this convention and an account of the retreat from the position he occupied in compliance with its articles.

Under date of the 25th June the Mexican Secretary at War writes to General Filisola, that he had communicated his despatches to the President of Mexico ad interim, and that their contents had excited his profound indignation. That he would be called before a Court Martial to account for not having remained in positions which he had been ordered to retain at every hazard, and for having obeyed the orders of the commanding general, though he was a prisoner. That the President ad interim will not recognize the convention concluded at Velasco on the 14th May, 1836, (that between Santa Anna and President Burnet) the General who signed it having no power to do so. That he expressly disapproves, as an attack on the rights of the nation, the title of republic, given to an insurgent department of Mexico, and that of President, to the chief of the insurgents. In conclusion the Secretary orders General Filisola to surrender the command to General Jose Urrea, and to repair to the city of Mexico to answer for his conduct.

There does not appear as yet to have been any serious disturbance in any part of the Mexican Republic; though from various editorial remarks the public mind is evidentially ill at ease.

THE LOUISIANA ADVERTISER

LATE FROM TEXAS

We learn that the Mexican forces on the Rio Grande, amount to 10,000 men, and that the Texian army were at present quartered at Labadie, to which place they had retired for the purpose of collecting the remains of the murdered men belonging to Fannin's detachment, and giving them a decent interment. — This they effected, much to the gratification of the surrounding inhabitants and volunteers.

The captive Santa Anna, (in irons) has been removed from Col-umbus to Labadie, where the main body of the army are stationed. The cause of his removal was owing to the late proceeding of the Cabinet, which was to the effect that he should be discharged, but it was counteracted by the people. There was also a rumor very current at Velasco, that the Mexicans intended to make a descent by sea upon Velasco to secure Santa Anna at all events, if retained there; but if such be their intentions they will be frustrated by the above removal.

NEW YORK DAILY ADVERTISER
TEXAS - BURIAL OF THE DEAD

The bodies of Col. Fannin's detachment, who were massacred in cold blood, were buried on the 3d June by the Texians, with military honors. An address was delivered on the occasion by Gen. Rusk. An official report of his proceedings has been communicated to and published by the Texian government, from which we make the following extracts: —

LA BAHIA, June 4th, 1836.

On our arrival at this place we found no difficulty in discovering the ground where Fannin and his gallant band were shot by order of Santa Anna. — Most of their bodies were burned, yet there were many bones and some entire skeletons scattered over the plains for some distance. It had long been determined that as soon as practicable after the arrival of our army here, their remains should be collected and a day set apart for their burial with all the honors of war. Accordingly, on Wednesday Gen. Rusk issued the following order:

"As a token of respect as well to the memory of the men who fell here a sacrifice to the treachery and bad faith of our enemy as a duty which we owe to the relations of the unfortunate deceased and ourselves, it is ordered that the skeletons and bones of our murdered countrymen be collected into one place in front of the fort and buried with all the honors of war."

The remains of the massacred troops were accordingly collected together on the 2d inst. The following morning the army were paraded within the walls of the fort at the hour appointed, and at 9 o'clock, with arms reversed the procession moved slowly towards the place of burial. On reaching the grave, Gen. Rusk delivered the following address:

"Fellow Soldiers — In the order of Providence, we are this day called upon to pay the last sad office of respect to the remains of the noble and heroic band, who battling for our sacred rights, have fallen beneath the ruthless hand of a tyrant.

"Their chivalrous conduct entitled them to the heartfelt gratitude of the people of Texas. Without any further interest in the country than that which all noble hearts feel at the bare mention of liberty, they rallied to our standard, relinquishing the ease, peace and comfort of their homes — leaving behind them all they held dear, their mothers, sisters, daughters and wives — they subjected themselves to fatigue and privation, and nobly threw themselves between the people of Texas and the legions of Santa Anna. Here, unaided by reinforcements and far from help and hope, they battled bravely with the minions of a tyrant ten to one.

Surrounded in the open prairie by the fearful odds, cut off from provisions and even water; they were induced under the promise of receiving treatment usual to prisoners of war to surrender. They were marched back and for a week treated with the utmost inhumanity and barbarity. They were

TEXAS — BURIAL OF THE DEAD
(CONTINUED)

marched out of yonder Fort, under the pretence of getting provisions, and it was not until the firing of musketry, and the shrieks of the dying, that they were notified of their approaching fate. — Some endeavored to make their escape, but they were pursued by the ruthless cavalry, and most of them cut down with their swords.

"A small number of them now stand by the grave, a bare remnant of that noble band. Our tribute of respect is due to them. It is due to the mothers, sisters and wives who weep their untimely end, that we should mingle our tears with theirs. In that mass of bones and fragments of bones, many a mother might see her son, many a sister her brother, and many a wife her once beloved and affectionate husband. But we have a consolation yet to offer them. Their murderers

sank into death, on the plains of San Jacinto, under the appalling words "Remember La Bahia."

"Many a tender affectionate woman will remember La Bahia. But we have another consolation to offer — it is, that while liberty has a habitation and a name, their chivalrous deeds will be handed down upon the bright pages of history.

"We can still offer another consolation. Santa Anna, the mock hero, the black hearted murderer, is within our grasp. Yea, and here he must remain tortured with the keen pains of corroding conscience. He must often remember La Bahia. And while the names of those whom he murdered shall soar to the highest pinnacle of fame, he shall sink into the lowest depths of infamy and disgrace."

119

NEW ORLEANS BULLETIN

ADDRESS OF GEN. LAMAR TO THE ARMY OF TEXAS

Soldiers of Texas:

On assuming the glorious responsibility of leading you to the field of battle, I am deeply impressed with gratitude for the trust confided; and feel most vividly, that to command an army of heroes in the cause of freedom is the highest of all privileges, and to conduct it to victory is the most enduring and exalting honor.

The enemy who so recently retired, terrified from our borders, are about to countermarch upon us with reinforcements formidable in count, but feeble in spirit and puissance. They come for the hellish purpose of desolating the loveliest of a thousand lands, and staining our luxuriant fields with blood of the cultivators.

Confident of numbers, they hope to gain by overwhelming force that which they cannot achieve by valor. They boast that they will retrieve the late inglorious defeat of their arms, or perish in the attempt; that they will drive us beyond the Sabine, or give us a grave this side. You, soldiers, know the futility of their vain-glorious boastings, as well as the ferocious character of their warfare.

Their cruelty and perfidy were sufficiently exemplified in their horrid massacres at Bexar and La Bahia, whilst their shameful route and discomfiture at the San Jacinto stand as a perpetual monument of their unexampled pusillanimity and dastardly conduct. Audacious monsters! That they have the willingness to murder is apparent — their ability to conquer, they never have shown. Their numbers can avail them nothing; and their threats of extermination, instead of intimidating, only invigorate the nerves of the bold and free. Let them come. — Their return is hailed with joy by every manly voice in Texas.

Another opportunity is afforded to vindicate our rights and avenge our wrongs. The greater the force, the richer the harvest! Though every blade of grass on the banks of the Rio Bravo bristle into a bayonet, it shall not save them. The very glance of a freeman's eye, is a blazing shield of Perseus to the monsters tyranny. They have to fly, or fall, before the wrath of an injured people, nerved in the cause of liberty and vengenance.

Soldiers! — Your country calls you to her defence. Your homes, your firesides — the scenes of your former joys, and future anticipations; all the endearments of domestic happiness, and all the hopes of future competence and peace, summon you to the field. You are summoned, too, by the spirit of Travis and Fannin and their gallant companions, whose blood has cemented the foundations of our freedom. Their flesh has been food for the raven, and their bones have been whitening on the prairies, until your pious patriotism gathered those scattered relics, with decent depulchral honors, to a soldier's grave. But their glorified spirits still hovering around the home of their patriotic devotion, call upon you to sustain the independence which they have consecrated by their martydom, and to recompense with merited vengenance, the wrongs they have endured from a perfidious and dastard enemy. Shall the call be made in vain? Shall we turn a deaf ear to the voice of our country, and the beseeching cries of our murdered brethren? Surely there can be no one so insensible to guilt and shame as to look with indifference upon the desolation of his country. If there be so foul a blot upon humanity — if there be one in the whole limits of our land who is mean enough when his home is invaded by an insolent foe, to seek safety in dishonorable flight. I would say to him, — Detested recreant! retire to the shades of infamy, and sully no more a beautiful land, whose blessings belong to the brave and virtuous. Let then every patriot and soldier every worthy citizen, who abhors the name of traitor, and condemns the vile epithet of coward, rally to the call promptly, around the unfurled banner of freedom — let him repair with impatient zeal to the theatre of his nation's glory, and there snatch upon the brink of danger, fame for himself and safety for his country. The dastard who lingers behind may fatten upon the fruits of his recreancy, but when he dies he rots in infamy, to the joy of all — whilst the noble hero who makes his bosom the bulwark of a people's liberty, will find a rich reward for toil and valor in the thanks of a grateful land, and the smiles of its high-toned beauty. If he fall in the holy cause he will still survive in the affection of his comrades, and his name will gather glory with the flight of ages —

Citizens of the Red Lands! You are looked to for aid in this second struggle for independence. Your contributions, herefore, have not been proportionate to your population. Few of you have participated in the toils and glory of the strife. Your homes have been exempt for the calamities of war. For that exemption you are indebted to the gallentry of your more exposed and suffering countrymen. Whatever circumstances may have restrained you before, there can remain no reasons to withhold you now. — We know your courage. Your skill in arms is familiar to us all. Your country requires the immediate exhibition of both, let both be displayed when the great and decisive battle which is pending shall be fought — and Texas is free, sovereign and independent! Hold not back, I adjure you, by every principal of honor, of gratitude, and of patriotism. If any man amongst you prove recreant now, let him be stigmatized, treat him as an outcast; and let a nation's contempt rest like a black cloud upon his name. The call, let all obey, and all will be well.

MIRABEAU B. LAMAR

Major-General Com.
the Army of Texas

Velesco, June 27, 1836.

NEW ORLEANS AMERICAN
FROM TEXAS

By the arrival from Texas yesterday morning, it appears that there is little likelihood of an engagement between the contending parties. The advance guard of either army, it is believed, are not within one hundred and fifty miles of each other, and there was scarcely any probability of the Mexican army advancing, as they were short of provisions and every munition of war: it will be recollected that their supplies were cut off by the interception and capture by the Texian armed cruisers.

Our informant states, that a few days before he left Texas, there was much indignation expressed among the soldiers against Santa Anna — and that they had made an attempt to shoot him, but were prevented by the timely interference of his guards. A pistol shot was fired at Santa Anna, but did him no injury. The excitement rose from the fact of the return of the Mexican army into Texas. To prevent any harm reaching him from the soldiery, his guard has been doubled.

The Texian force is estimated at about 3000 men, but from the number of volunteers flocking in, especially from the western and southern states, it was presumed that in a few weeks, it would be augmented to 6000 men. Cos, and other officers, with about 400 prisoners, are at Galveston Island. It is said to be the intention of the Texians, in case the Mexicans attack them, to put all the prisoners to the sword.

It is rumored that Santa Anna had written to President Jackson, asking him, or the government, to be his security for any treaty he may enter into with the Texians. He is said to have informed that they have no reason to apprehend an attack from his countrymen, as he would issue a proclamation that would induce them to evacuate without striking a single blow. The Texians, however, appear to put but little confidence in his word and are preparing for every exigency. They are well supplied with provisions and munitions of war, and we are informed would rather fight than not.

General Houston had not arrived when the Shenandoah sailed. Lamar is appointed commander-in-chief in his absence, it is supposed that he would resign on his return.

A few days previous to the departure of the Shenandoah, an individual, by the name of Barts, died at Columbia. The general presumption was, that his real name was Bartow, the cashier of the Albany, New York Bank, who absconded sometime since, in consequence of the depredations which he committed while a cashier of that institution. He had in his possession fifteen thousand dollars.

Dr. Archer is confidently spoken of as the next President of Texas, to succeed Burnet, who is daily becoming more unpopular.

The schooner Julius Ceasar, was loaded and ready to sail.

THE NEW ORLEANS BEE

TEXAS

By the schooner Julius Ceasar, which arrived yesterday from Texas, we have information which renders it very doubtful whether the Mexican army will really prosecute further operations, for the present at least, in Texas.

From Texian spies sent for the purpose of reconnoitering the enemy, it is ascertained that the Mexican had not advanced, and that its numbers are continually diminishing by desertion. Santa Anna had solicited by letter the amicable interposition of President Jackson, and had conveyed to the Mexican government his opinion that the conquest of Texas was impossible, and that the independence of Texas should be recognized.

The schooner Brutus, was at Matagorda, blockaded by the Mexican brig of war Vencedor del Alamo, but would soon be relieved by the schooner Invincible, Union, and other vessels that had proceeded there in tow of the steamboat Ocean, for the purpose of capturing the brig. The steamboat was laden with volunteers, and for her protection there was raised a breastwork of cotton bales.

THE TROY DAILY WHIG

IMPORTANT FROM MEXICO AND TEXAS

By a late arrival at N.Y. from New Orleans, intelligence has been received from Mexico and Texas of a highly important and interesting character. It appears that great dissensions prevail not only in the Capital, but in all the Mexican States. These troubles grow out of the struggle for power between the friends and enemies of Santa Anna and have produced various revolutionary movements in the several provinces having for their object the prostration of the "Central Despotism" heretofore upheld by the strong arm of military force and the establishment of a Federation or Republican Government. If these accounts are to be relied on, the Mexicans will have abundance of occupation for their troops at home and will be obliged to countermarch from Texas into their own territory. The course of events is now most decidedly in favor of the cause of Texas. The Mexican Congress were discussing at the last advices the treaty entered into at San Jacinto between General Houston and Santa Anna.

The following letter, dated Matamoras, is published in the New Orleans Bulletin:

Dear Sir — Through the medium of your paper I think it highly necessary that the government of the United States, as well as the Texians, should be informed of what presented itself, so odious, in my opinion, in the character of General Urrea, the Mexican commander-in-chief, too unpardonable to be overlooked, and should be immediately attended to by the United States.

We have at this moment six or seven Indian chiefs, Cherokees and other tribes, with their interpreters, from Texas. These Indians are on a mission to the general, and have had several private meetings with him. There exists no doubt of the business they have come on, and have made propositions to the general to join the Mexicans against the Texians, which appears now to be concluded, as Col. Waterchea is to be despatched tomorrow to their camp, some distance up the river, where they have 30 or 40 in number, to be used as spies or runners. I had occasion to call on General Urrea, at headquarters on business, when I met there three of the Indians, with their interpreters, making inquiries of the strength of their tribe. The general being anxious to ascertain what force they could muster with the other tribes.

The commissary of this place has orders to purchase eight hundred or a thousand horses for the cavalry, which he is now doing. Every movement appears to confirm the belief that the negotiation is concluded with a promise to the Indians of land and cattle, should they assist and succeed in exterminating the population of Texas.

Public tranquility continues to be preserved here: but the general opinion seems to be, that our present government is not likely to last long, and that another attempt will be made soon, to return to the Federal System of the government.

From the New York papers, it appears that the Mexican army was

IMPORTANT FROM MEXICO AND TEXAS
(CONTINUED)

still at Matamoras, but in poor condition, and diminishing rapidly by desertion.

General Houston had not yet rejoined the Texian army.

LATER FROM MEXICO AND TEXAS

Intelligence has been received at N.Y. from Mexico — all is vague and uncertain in that country. They represent everything as peaceful in the city of Mexico as well as in the different states. In contradiction to these statements, the measures taken by the government, betray the greatest fears of insubordination and revolt.

General Filisola had reached the capital and had surrendered himself for trial.

125

NEW ORLEANS
COMMERCIAL BULLETIN

LATEST FROM TEXAS

We here print a letter from a gentleman now in Texas, which gives some interesting information as to the present and future movements. It is dated Velasco, July 20, 1836.

Our army is still at Victoria, upon the Guadaloupe. Lamar had arrived there agreeably to the last accounts, and presented himself as Commander-in-Chief of the Texain forces; but with all his popularity was unable to obtain the concurrence of the army with the wishes of the cabinet. The question was put to a vote, whether he should enjoy the chief command, or Rusk to continue in his former capacity, until the arrival of General Houston. The matter was decided by an ooverwhelming majority in favor of the two latter gentlemen; so that Rusk continues as Brigadier General commanding, and the authority of Major General Houston will be recognized as soon as he arrives in camp. Lamar is said to have behaved in his usual disinterested and patriotic manner.

The army in the field at this time is 2000 strong. The whole country is up and moving on to camp. The old settlers are determined to redeem their injured credit, — undeservedly injured, as the great majority of them could not have acted differently, and secured their families from the blood thirsty violence of a ruthless and semi-barbarous foe, — and they are now flocking onward, to prove to an invidious world that their arms are as strong, and the spirit of liberty burning as brightly in their hearts, as it ever did in the olden time,

when the independence of their mother country was in it's cradle, and rocking amid the elements of internal discord and foreign recklessness.

Felix Houston has been promoted to the rank of Brigadier General by brevet. Green still enjoys the commission which he appeared to prize so highly in New Orleans. They are now both in camp. Santa Anna, the ill fated despot, is now at Columbia, and has the pleasing anticipation of shortly being escorted to the army, and there receiving his sentence — a detachment has been ordered in for that purpose. You may hear of a catastrophe before many weeks have passed. I anticipate it with positive certainty. Miserable indecision in not having inflicted upon him "death or worse punishment" immediately after his capture, when the act would have been upheld and justified by the whole civilized world.

General Rusk ordered the Mexican families on the Guadaloupe and La Baca, and all those likely to afford information to the enemy, to retire upon the Rio Grande, or take themselves off to the Colorado.

There is said to be no more Mexican troops this side of the Rio Grande. They are preparing to make a desperate effort to heal their wounded honor, and recover possession of this paradise. That they are calling up all their resources, and at this moment straining every nerve for the purpose of making a sudden and formidable descent upon us, is too apparent to need substantiation. I am strongly inclined to believe that their present intention is to make a combined and simultaneous attack by land and sea.

At all events we should be prepared for the crisis, and surely our friends in the United States will aid us in obtaining a sloop of war. I am obliged to break off here, as the vessel is just getting under weigh.

THE TROY DAILY WHIG

TEXAS

Extract of a letter from an officer in Texas to a gentleman in this city, dated Galveston Island, August 2nd, 1836. — I think we are in a fair way for peace now in Texas. There was a reaction by the Mexicans at one time, after their defeated army retired to the Rio Grande, and an attempt was made to reinforce, to make another invasion upon us; but all so far has proved a failer, or likely to do so, in consequence of some internal commotions in Mexico. I think we shall have no further trouble with the Mexicans, yet our volunteers are anxious to "go ahead". Our army is 2,500 strong, and increasing daily, in high spirits, ready for the contest.

My rendezvous is at Galveston Island, where I am in command at present. All the Mexican officers, except Santa Anna and Almonte, and most of the private soldiers are here, my prisoners. I am fortifying and going ahead here. I have been expecting an attack daily, but now believe the danger is over.

THE NEW ORLEANS
TRUE AMERICAN

LATE FROM TEXAS

By the arrival late yesterday of the schooner San Jacinto, 3 days from Galveston, we learn that the Mexican schooner Matilda, which had been captured by the Texian schooner of war Terrible, arrived there under the charge of a prize master. She was bound from Sisal Champeachy, with a cargo of limes, flour, corn, beans, and cigars.

The Terrible had pursued and driven onto shore a Mexican schooner which was lost; name not recollected.

The schooner Urchin, brigs Durango and Good Hope, had left Galveston for Matagorda with troops. 3,000 Texians, under General Rusk, were marching to Matamoras to take possession thereof.

Colonel Mehia, one of the prisoners captured at San Jacinto, died at Galveston.

We have to acknowledge the reciept of a letter under the date of Galveston, July 9th, 1836, from W. P. Bradburn, one of the Kentucky volunteers, who left the city some weeks since, in the schooner Flash. The volunteers are represented to be in good spirits, and resolved never to see the flag, presented to them by the ladies of Kentucky, in the hands of the bloody Mexicans! Most of the information which this letter contains in relation to Texas, had been anticipated by previous arrivals. It is said, however, that General Houston is spoken of as the next President.

THE NEW YORK STAR

SANTA ANNA AND ALMONTE

These prisoners were, it appears, still at Columbia, July 29th. Their fate is uncertain. They may be spared, but the tide of opinion is more against them then it was.

So far from the Mexican troops concentrating at Matamoras to invade Texas, the belief is they have scattered and disbanded in various directions.

THE CINCINATTI WHIG

!!CHARGE OF TREASON AGAINST THE PRESIDENT OF TEXAS!!

A captain of the Texian army, now in this city, directly from Texas, informs us that charges had been formally preferred against Mr. Burnet, the President of Texas, for treason. The charges were signed by nearly all the principal officers of the Texian army. His release of Santa Anna, and other suspicious acts, furnished the foundation for the accusation.

We do not for a moment believe that any charge against President Burnet injuriously affecting his moral principals, can be sustained. His integrity and patriotism are known by his friends to be beyond the reach of even detraction.

THE NEW YORK STAR

PRESIDENT BURNET -

The following extract from Brazoria Texas, dated Aug. 5th, 1836, explains the rumor of the arrest of Burnet —

"A Colonel Millard undertook to arrest the President, which produced a prodigious sensation — the people rose up in arms to oppose him, and he gave it up. General Rusk will have the Colonel arrested, and he no doubt, will loose his commission."

Millard is from New York.

Austin is confidently spoken of as the next President.

129

PHILADELPHIA INQUIRER

TEXAS

We learn from Capt. A. S. Lewis of the Texian army, who just left Gains' Ferry that the Mexican army was concentrating at Matamoros, and supposed to be 11,000 strong. This information, however, it will be seen by the later intelligence, there is reason to believe was erroneous.

The Texian army were 2500 strong, at Victoria, under Gen. Lamar, and the greatest spirit and unanimity prevailed among them. Gen. Houston was at St. Augustine, and was anxiously looked for. Santa Anna was at Columbia, under the charge of Major Patton; he was to be sent to the vicinity of the Sabine, to be regularly tried. The Texians were generally in favor of preserving his life, provided the Mexicans made no further incursions into Texas.

Capt. Lewis himself was one of the officers of a company that had Santa Anna, Cos, and Almonte in charge for several weeks. He had frequent and free conversations with each of them. Santa Anna, he describes, as a very fine looking man — unable to speak English with any degree of fluency — and in very low spirits, conscious that his life will be taken the moment his countrymen re-march upon his captors. Cos expects death and is prepared to meet his fate with some degree of fortitude. Almonte is a polished man— converses very fluently in English, and is rather a favorite than otherwise with the army, as he never committed any direct act of atrocity, but merely acted like hundreds of others in the service of Santa Anna.

The crops throughout Texas are very abundant — much more so than could have been expected, as little attention, was paid to them. The army was fully provided with provisions — and it was believed that little suffering would be experienced on this score, should the Mexicans march against them. Recruits were constantly pouring in.

Capt. Lewis believes that an army of even 15,000 Mexicans could not conquer Texas, against one-fourth the number of Americans. The Mexicans are miserable troops, and, moreover, disheartened by their terrible defeat at San Jacinto. It is certain that the Indians are disposed to join the Mexicans. The principal and ruling tribe, and who are at the same time the most numerous, are the Cherokees, who count 2000 warriors, which, with the smaller tribes, would make 4000 — the whole of which are at the disposition of a talented chief names Bowles, to his disgrace an AMERICAN, who has married a squaw of some distinction. He is exciting the Indians against his countrymen.

THE NEW ORLEANS TRUE AMERICAN

TEXAS

"Congress was to meet on the first Monday in October in the town of Columbia. The army 2200 strong is at Coleto, near Copano; its numbers have been considerably reduced in consequence of many of the Texians having returned to the cultivation of their farms. It is understood that the expedition to Matamoras has been abandoned, and thus there is no prospect of a meeting of the two armies until winter. Santa Anna has been sent to the plantation of Col. Phelps under a strong guard."

NEW ORLEANS BULLETIN

!!ATTEMPT TO RESCUE SANTA ANNA!!

By the Ceasar, an armed Texas warship, we also learn of the abortion of a plan concocted in our goodly city, for the purpose of rescuing from his thralldom, Santa Anna. The selfsytled second Napoleon is still, however, in durance vile, and eager desire of his friends to release him therefrom, has only added to the greater security of his person.

Several individuals, it seems, recently left our city in the schooner Passaic, with a view to effect the deliverance of the captive, and by placing him on board transport him to some place of destination. All concerned, however, have been arrested on the charge and will themselves most probably be made to endure a confinement, not by any means calculated to enlist the sympathies of their countrymen.

Mexican gold may do much, and has brought out instruments base enough to attempt the liberation of a man, who has proved himself unworthy of the name, but has not as yet, and will not succeed in lulling to sleep the Augusteyed vigilance of those who love their country, and have within their power its most deadly enemy.

The captain and crew of the schooner Passaic, it is stated, in a letter from Brazoria, has been apprehended on a charge of being concerned in a plot to effect the deliverance of Santa Anna.

NEW YORK
COURIER AND INQUIRER

SANTA ANNA AND ALMONTE

From the schooner Congress, from Velasco, Texas, we learn that Santa Anna and Almonte had been relieved of their irons. A treaty was negociating between the former and the Cabinet, the object of which, according to the best information, is to re-establish the Federal System of Government in Mexico, with the acknowledgement of the independence of Texas. Santa Anna has promised to effect this remarkable change through the medium of some of his proteges and well tried adherents, who are yet in command of Mexico, and who, no doubt will obey his orders and directions. But he himself shall not recover his liberty until the treaty has received it's full execution. There is no doubt that the Texas war will ultimately be terminated by one of these agreements, and then a new era will begin in that Republic.

THE NEW YORK EVENING POST

HIGHLY IMPORTANT FROM TEXAS!
HOUSTON ELECTED PRESIDENT!
ANOTHER ATTEMPT MADE
TO RESCUE SANTA ANNA!

A vessel arrived from Galveston, by which information is received that Houston has been elected President of Texas, and that another fruitless attempt has been made by a Spaniard, of the name of Payes, to rescue Santa Anna. He stated that he was employed for the purpose by the Mexican Consul at New Orleans; this however is doubtless void of all foundation.

The armed Texian schooner Terrible had taken several Mexican prizes, which were sent in for adjudication.

The Texian army, about 3000 strong, had removed their camp, to the Garcite, near Matagorda Bay.

132

THE NEW ORLEANS BEE

INFORMATION FROM THE INTERIOR

Mr. Peter Suzeman, a gentleman of considerable intelligence, arrived here a few days since, direct from Matamoras. He says the Mexicans has, by desertion, been reduced to about 2200 men, that they are in a miserable situation. Urrea was still in command. Andrade has left for the south. Mr. S. says he is confident no campaign will be made against Texas this year, and he doubts very much whether the Mexican nation will consider it politic ever to make another. He confirms the report of a revolution having broken out in the interior, and says that General Valencia had been proclaimed Dictator by the military. He also states that Generals Sesma and Filisola had been arrested and tried by a Court Martial for cowardice and mismanagement in the Texas campaign, and that the latter had been condemned to be shot. He represents the feelings of the foreigners in Matamoras, as decidedly in our favor, and says that in the event of a campaign against that place they would unite with Texas.

The Texain schooner of war Invincible, returned a few days ago from a cruise along the coast of Mexico, without meeting with a single armed Mexican vessel.

The Invincible sent in a challenge to a Mexican brig of war El Vencedor del Alamo, which was not accepted on the pretext that the crews of the challenged, were not in condition to fight for want of pay.

The Invincible crew landed at the river St. John and St. Paul, where they compelled the Mexican inhabitants to bring them wood and water.

THE NEW ORLEANS BULLETIN

LATEST FROM TEXAS

By the arrival of the schooner Pennsylvania, yesterday, from Velasco, Texas, we are in possession of news from that country. So little dread of an enemy prevails in the country at present, that the people are quitely cultivating their lands, and attending, it would seem, theatrical performances. Some theatrical corps have opened the temple and made a debut at Columbia, under favorable auspices. The army remains stationary, and somewhat impatient to be engaged in military duty, in which, notwithstanding threats of formidable preparations on the part of their enemies, we suspect they will be disappointed, as time will disclose. We, a long time since, prophecied that not another hostile gun would be fired in Texas, and as yet we have lost no faith in our prophetic gift in this particular.

The papers containing the proceedings of their newly organized congress, furnish no matter of great public interest, the members are yet engaged in regulating the matters of order and etiquette; prior to entering upon their more serious deliberations. Santa Anna is still in confinement which is rumored, not to be so rigid as of late, there being on foot some measures preparatory to his release. Should it be true, and he is to be released, Texas should require something in the way of a ransom, to enable her to discharge some of the heavy liabilities incurred by her belligerent operations.

NEW ORLEANS COMMERCIAL BULLETIN

MEXICAN TROOPS STILL DESERTING

The latest advices from Matamoras represents commerce at a stand-still. The Mexican troops are deserting for want of pay, clothing, food, and probably from some little indisposition to encounter the men of San Jacinto. General Urrea has resigned, and in fact everything wears a sorry aspect for the Mexican cause, while the Star of Texas is greatly on the ascendant.

We have been favored with the sight of a letter, dated Matamoras, Sept. 26, 1836, which represents things there as being very gloomy, business being dull and money uncommonly scarce — large amounts have been robbed on the road from Mexico.

General Urrea has resigned the command of the troops to General Amador. The troops have received no pay for a long time, and are still deserting the ranks very fast, still our informant adds, that they are well fed and clothed.

THE TROY DAILY WHIG

THE TEXAS REVOLUTION IN GENERAL

The causes which led to the revolution in Texas are a matter of history, and we do not desire at present to comment upon them. Nor do we wish to inquire whether the originators of this war were influenced by motives of patriotism, love of liberty, or by the "unregulated spirit of speculation." Such an analysis of motives would, to say the least of it, be invidious at this late hour. The blow has already been struck by bold hands of political adventurers, and Texas has been severed from the Mexican Government. Her independence has been proclaimed, and the contest for it's maintenance will certainly be successful. Yea, the struggle may, indeed, be protracted for years, but the efforts of Mexico to reduce Texas to a province of that Empire, will prove unavailing. This being the probable, nay, certain result of this war, the question then arises: what course does sound policy dictate as the most proper to be taken by the United States towards this new nation?

135

ABOUT THE ARTIST

JOSEPH HEFTER: American citizen of German descent, born 1898, at present living in retirement in Mexico. Devoted 40 years partly or wholly to research or study of military history as author, editor, translator and illustrator of documented articles, books and plates on this subject. The last ten years were dedicated to a systematic effort to investigate directly at Mexican sources, evidence related to early Southwest history, from the Spanish colonial period to the Texas War of Independence and the Mexican-American War, comparing documents and writings in Spain, Mexico and the United States, in order to clear up discrepancies and contradictions accumulated over the years. Some of these studies were published in the form of books, plates, articles, translations, and collaborations, among them:

"The Mexican Soldier 1837-1847", "The Insurgents of 1810"; "The San Blas Battalion 1825-1855"; "Pictorial Bibliography of Spanish Military Dress"; Appendix to "The Siege And Taking Of The Alamo"; essays in 'Texas Military History' such as "The Texan Naval Raid on Silan, 1837"; "The Riddle Of The Alamo Battle Flag 1836"; "Uniforms Of The Coahuila-Texas Civic Militia of 1834"; "Texas and the War With Mexico" and "The Great West" in the 'American Heritage' series; Santa Anna's Defence of the Capital of the Republic 1847" and several others.

In addition to these written studies, the even more difficult task was undertaken of reconstructing in drawings and paintings, a picture record of these early Texas and Mexican events, and of the men who took part in them. The recent "Chronicle of Mexican Military Dress From the XVI to the XX Century" with .. language text, profusely illustrated and published within the renowned 'Artes de Mexico' series, covers a hitherto completely neglected subject. The widely known series of hand-colored plates 'Military Uniforms in America' includes reconstructions of "The Cuera Dragoon 1730-1830"; "The Spanish Texas Hussars 1803"; "The Mexican Spy Company 1846", "A Spanish Presidio Visitador 1720" and a number of others. A further set of color drawings recreated "The Uniforms of the Texas Republic Army of 1839" and "Scouts of the Ugalde Expedition to Texas 1787-88".

An interesting opportunity presented itself when Mr. Jerry J. Gaddy of Pasadena, Texas, enthusiastic researcher and collector of early Texana, conceived the idea of a series of paintings, bringing to life the Alamo-San Jacinto period as seen from the Mexican side and based on Mexican sources. This resulted in a set of tempera paintings: "Santa Anna's Staff Conference in Front of the Alamo, March 5th. 1836"; "The Assult on the Alamo March 6th. 1836 5 A.M."; "The Fall of the Alamo March 6th. 1836 8 A.M."; "San Jacinto, 21 April 1836, 4:15 P.M."; and twin panels "A Mexican Soldier in Texas 1836" and "A Texan Independence Fighter 1836". It took more than 2 years of preliminary research, cross-checking and actual work to complete these scenes, but they throw a slightly more accurate light on this hectic and heroic period, bringing it closer to the minds and hearts of Texas history lovers.

137

ACKNOWLEDGEMENTS

Personally, I have seldom bothered myself with reading the "AC-KNOWLEDGEMENTS" section in various books, possibly because, before this, I thought the people listed there were simply good friends of the writer, or maybe, I reasoned, the writer felt that if the book never sold to anyone else, at least the people listed there would buy a copy. Alas, how wrong I was!

Also, until the time I began to put this work together I felt that nothing could be quite so simple as compiling a group of newspaper accounts and molding them into book form. I discovered quickly that this, too, was a mistake. Nothing is simple, and certainly no one person can effectivly attack the problems involved in a project of this type.

With the above in mind I would like to introduce the reader to only a few of the many that made my work so much easier.

Since I have never seen the publisher of a book given thanks, I must wonder if this is taboo, or, at best, "simply not an accepted practice." This book was begun on an unusual format, so perhaps it is fitting that it also end in that vain.

M. J. Koury, the publisher of this book has shown faith to an un-proven Texas writer, whose biggest desire to date has been to bring these accounts to the attention of the readers of Texana. He has recognized that a book dealing with a newspaper account of the Texas revolution has never been attempted, and yet, as publisher of, THE OLD ARMY PRESS, he musters the necessary courage and goes to press. Whether the practice of thanking one's publisher is frowned upon or not, I find it most necessary in this instance.

Perhaps the greatest influence of all has been the advice and help I have received from Joseph Hefter, of Mexico City. In no small way has this learned man assisted me in compiling, checking and cross-checking the events contained here. His art work is without peers, as the reader will surely testify by the color plates contained in these pages. These paintings are the result of over two years of research, which should give the viewer some idea of Mr. Hefter's drive for both accuracy and historical awareness. Certainly many discussions wiill arise that deal with these paintings, and so it should be, for Mr. Hefter has presented these for more than the simple purpose of viewing; he has built into this group of paintings all the characteristics that should be found in works of this type: accuracy, detail, and thought provoking ideas that will make even the most astute historians wonder at their own conclusions. After delving into history for more than forty years, as Mr. Hefter has done, it's almost certain that many years will pass before our contemporary historians can, if indeed, at all, come forth and attempt to surpass his works. Their efforts should prove interesting.

The late Walter Lundquist, of New Jersey, started his program of, "HELP A TEXAN," as he referred to it, in 1964. Walt, more than anyone else is responsible for the accounts contained here, but more than that, he was a friend who showed me the way to many news items that would have surely gone un-noticed by me. He had a keen eye for catching obscure articles and bringing them to my attention. It is sad, indeed, that Walt could not have been here to see this book in print.

138

Mrs. Barbara Stuhlmuller, Editor and Publisher of "THE NEWSPAPER COLLECTORS GAZETTE," is another of the many people who gave freely of both time and news accounts. While I may never really know the number of hours this lady donated in my behalf, I know they were considerable.

Newspaper collectors and dealers from many parts of the United States have contributed to this work. Among which I must include; Walter Dougherty, Joe Bowes, M. S. Devins, J. M. Craig, C. D. David, George Hart, and a host of others.

To the people listed above, and the many, many others that space will not allow, I offer you, my friends, my sincerest thanks, and hope the end result has been worth your time and talents.

THE SCOURCES:

NEW YORK COURIER AND INQUIRER
THE TROY DAILY WHIG
NEW ORLEANS TRUE AMERICAN
THE NEW YORK AMERICAN
NEW ORLEANS BEE
THE RED RIVER HERALD
JOURNAL OF COMMERCE
THE BALTIMORE GAZETTE
MOBILE CHRONICAL
NEW YORK COMMERCIAL ADVERTISER
NEW YORK MERCHANTILE ADVERTISER
NEW ORLEANS COMMERCIAL BULLETIN
THE NEW ORLEANS UNION
NEW YORK EVENING POST
NEW ORLEANS TEXIAN AGENCY
JACKSON TENNESSEE TRUTH TELLER
NEW ORLEANS COURIER
THE LOUISIANA ADVERTISER
THE LOUISVILLE JOURNAL
THE CINCINNATI WHIG
NEW YORK STAR
THE ALBANY ARGUS
THE PENSACOLA GAZETTE
ALBANY EVENING JOURNAL
NEW YORK DAILY ADVERTISER
PHILADELPHIA GAZETTE
THE PENNSYLVANIAN
THE NATIONAL INTELLIGENCER